DIVING & SNORKELING
Bonaire

Tim Rock

lonely planet

MELBOURNE | LONDON | OAKLAND

Bonaire

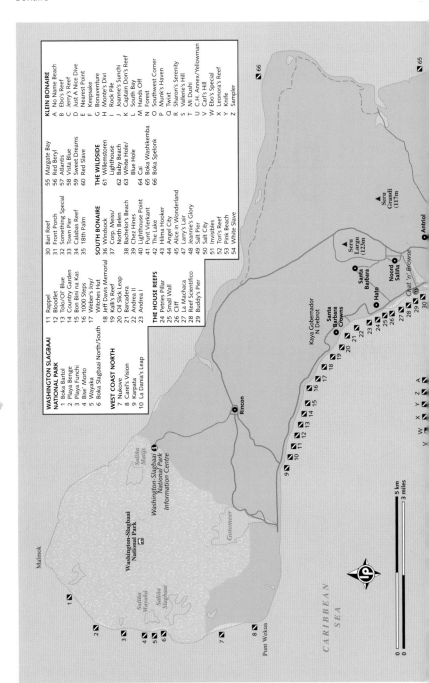

WASHINGTON SLAGBAAI NATIONAL PARK
1 Boka Bartol
2 Playa Benge
3 Playa Funchi
4 Bise' Morto
5 Wayaka
6 Boka Slagbaai North/South

WEST COAST NORTH
7 Nukove
8 Carel's Vision
9 Karpata
10 La Dania's Leap
11 Rappel
12 Bloodlet
13 Tolo/Ol' Blue
14 Country Garden
15 Bon Bini na Kas
16 1000 Steps
17 Weber's Joy/ Witches Hut
18 Jeff Davis Memorial
19 Kalli's Reef
20 Oil Slick Leap
21 Barcadera
22 Andrea II
23 Andrea I

THE HOUSE REEFS
24 Petries Pillar
25 Small Wall
26 Cliff
27 La Machaca
28 Reef Scientifico
29 Buddy's Pier
30 Bari Reef
31 Front Porch
32 Something Special
33 Town Pier
34 Calabas Reef
35 18th Palm

SOUTH BONAIRE
36 Windsock
37 Corp. Meiss/ North Belen
38 Bachelor's Beach
39 Chez Hines
40 Lighthouse Point
41 Punt Vierkant
42 The Lake
43 Hilma Hooker
44 Angel City
45 Alice in Wonderland
46 Larry's Lair
47 Jeannie's Glory
48 Salt Pier
49 Salt City
50 Invisibles
51 Tori's Reef
52 Pink Beach
53 White Slave

THE WILDSIDE
54 Willemstoren Lighthouse
55 Baby Beach
56 White Hole/ Blue Hole
57 Cai
58 Boka Washikemba
59 Boka Spelonk

55 Margate Bay
56 Red Beryl
57 Atlantis
58 Vista Blue
59 Sweet Dreams
60 Red Slave

61 Willemstoren Lighthouse
62 Baby Beach
63 White Hole/ Blue Hole
64 Cai
65 Boka Washikemba
66 Boka Spelonk

KLEIN BONAIRE
A No Name Beach
B Ebo's Reef
C Jerry's Reef
D Just A Nice Dive
E Nearest Point
F Keepsake
G Bonaventure
H Monte's Divi
I Rock Pile
J Joanne's Sunchi
K Captain Don's Reef
L South Bay
M Hands Off
N Forest
O Southwest Corner
P Munk's Haven
Q Twixt
R Sharon's Serenity
S Vallerie's Hill
T Mi Dushi
U C.H. Annex/Yellowman
V Carl's Hill
W Ebo's Special
X Leonora's Reef
Y Knife
Z Sampler

Malmok

Washington-Slagbaai National Park

Washington-Slagbaai National Park Information Centre

Salina Matijs

Salina Wayaka

Salina Slagbaai

Gotomeer

Rincon

Kaya Gobernador N Debrot

Santa Barbara Crowns

Santa Barbara

Hato

Seru Largu (123m)

Seru Grandi (117m)

Noord Salina

Chat 'n' Browse

Antriol

CARIBBEAN SEA

Punt Wakua

0   5 km
0   3 miles

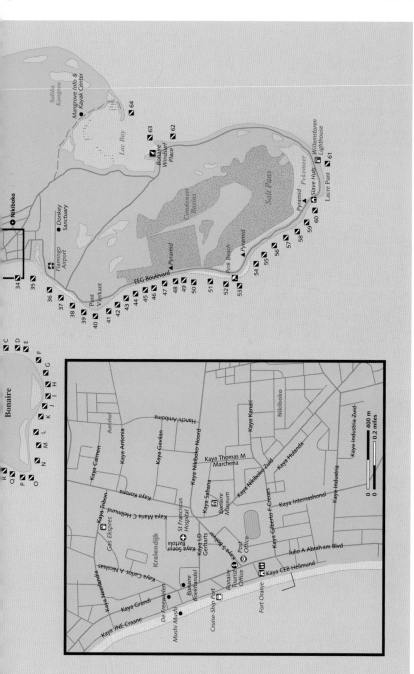

Bonaire

Nikiboko

Saliña Kangreu

Mangrove Info & Kayak Center

Lac Bay

63
62
64

Bonaire Windsurf Place

Donkey Sanctuary

Flamingo Airport

Condenser Basins

Salt Pans

Pekelmeer

Slave Huts

Willemstoren Lighthouse

Pyramid

Punt Vierkant

EEG Boulevard

Pink Beach

Pyramid

Pyramid

Lacre Punt

61

34
35
36
37
38
39
40
41
42
43
44
45
46
47
48
49
50
51
52
53
54
55
56
57
58
59
60

Kralendijk

Antriol

Hanchi Amboina

Kaya Catmen

Kaya Antonia

Kaya Gavilan

Kaya Korona

Kaya Nikiboko Noord

Kaya Thomas M Marchena

Kaya Kamari

Nikiboko

Kaya Tribon

Kaya Maria C Hellmund

St Franciscus Hospital

Kaya Sabana

Bonaire Museum

Kaya Nikiboko Zuid

Kaya Hulanda

Kaya Industria Zuid

Gas Ekspres

Kaya Carlos A Nicolaas

Kaya LD Gerharts

Kaya Soeur Bartola

Kaya S Bolivar

Post Office

Kaya Gilberto F Croes

Kaya Internashonal

Kaya Industria

Kaya Neerlandia

Bonaire Boekhandel

Bonaire Tourist Office

Julio A Abraham Blvd

De Freewieleri

Mushi Mushi

Kaya Grandi

Cruise-Ship Port

Fort Oranje

Kaya CEB Hellmund

Kaya JNE Craane

400 m
0.2 miles
0
0

Diving & Snorkeling Bonaire
2nd edition – September 2006

Published by
Lonely Planet Publications Pty Ltd
ABN 36 005 607 983
90 Maribyrnong St, Footscray,
Victoria, 3011, Australia
www.lonelyplanet.com

Lonely Planet Offices
Australia Locked Bag 1, Footscray, Victoria, 3011
Phone 03 8379 8000 Fax 03 8379 8111
Email talk2us@lonelyplanet.com.au

USA 150 Linden St, Oakland, CA 94607
Phone 510 893 8555 Toll free 800 275 8555 Fax 510 893 8572
Email info@lonelyplanet.com

UK 72-82 Rosebery Ave London EC1R 4RW
Phone 020 7841 9000 Fax 020 7841 9001
Email go@lonelyplanet.co.uk

Author Tim Rock
Publisher Roz Hopkins
Publishing Manager Chris Rennie
Commissioning Editor Ben Handicott
Design Manager Brendan Dempsey
Mapping Development Paul Piaia
Project Management Annelies Mertens
Production Pepper Publishing (Aust) Pty Ltd
Print Production Manager Graham Imeson

Printed by C&C Offset Printing Co Ltd, China
Photographs Tim Rock (unless otherwise noted)

ISBN 1864501219

With Many Thanks to
Jennifer Bilos, Jo Vraca, Alison Lyall, Carol Chandler, Amy Carroll,
Angus Fleetwood, Tom Calderwood, Sayher Heffernan

Contents

A big school of snapper congregate
at reeftop on Bonaire's Wildside

Author

TIM ROCK

Tim Rock attended the journalism program at the University of Nebraska at Omaha and has been a broadcast and print photojournalist for 30 years. The majority of those years has been spent in the Western and Indo Pacific reporting on environmental and conservation issues.

His television series, *Aquaquest Micronesia,* was an Ace Award finalist. He has also produced six documentaries on the history and undersea fauna of the region. Rock won the prestigious Excellence in the Use of Photography from the Society of Publishers in Asia. He also has many other awards for photography and writing, publishes a magazine and is a correspondent for numerous Pacific Rim magazines. He is the author of six other Lonely Planet series guides, including *Chuuk Lagoon, Pohnpei & Kosrae, Bali & Lombok, Guam & Yap, Palau, South Africa* and *Papua New Guinea,* and is a major contributor to *Philippines.* Lonely Planet Images (www.lonelyplanetimages.com) and other agents worldwide represent Rock's photographic work.

FROM THE AUTHOR

Thank you to my wife Larie for her continued support and for holding down the fort while I travel. Olga Spoelstra provided her many talents and unselfish help and friendship in making images and words for this book. Anne Louise Tuke shared some great insights about her beloved Bonaire. Also, Capt Don Stewart, Janet Thibault, Larry Baillie, Janice Huckaby, Martin Heinrich, Jackson Winkler, Martijn Eichhorn and Monique Reichert, Simone Wackenhut, Jack and Karen Chalk, Harley Chalk, Chris Chalk, George Buckley, Dee Scarr, Ernesto 'Netto' Bernabella, Jenny Marchena, Christina Wooten, Karen Pearson, Max Margarita, Rozaida Rosaria, Bous Scholtz, Ronella Croes, George Thode, Fernando Simal, Rolando Marin, Ramon de Leon, Elsmarie Beukenboom, BNMP and STINAPA staff and the people of Bonaire for their hospitality and dedication to the preservation of the marine world that surrounds their beautiful island.

FROM THE PUBLISHER

Bonaire is one of diving's special places. The island and its people have dedicated themselves to the conservation of its reefs and resources. We are happy to present this new guide to the snorkel and dive sites of the island and hope you enjoy its bountiful natural resources.

PHOTO NOTES

Tim Rock uses Aquatica housings and Canon 20D cameras with Canon and Sigma lenses. Ikelite makes his DS125 strobes. TLC strobe arms are used to angle the strobes. Land cameras are also Canon, with Canon, Sigma and Tamron lenses. All photos are by the author unless otherwise noted.

Introduction

The island of Bonaire is one of those places that claims to be a diver's paradise. It even says so on the license plates. This may seem to be too broad of a claim, but divers are seen at just about every venue on the island at any time of the day.

One of the true environmental success stories – not only in the diving world but internationally, the entire reef system around the island and satellite island Klein Bonaire is a national park. Everything on the reef is protected and every effort is made to keep the reefs healthy. The people of Bonaire have been stewarding the reefs for decades and they have become a source of national pride.

Part of the ABC islands of Aruba, Bonaire and Curaçao, this island has tried to keep an individual identity in the southern Caribbean. Inhabited by residents who have a rough history first as slaves and then as farmers in an arid land, they are an independent lot, happy to be on their own and away from the political squabbles in the more populous Curaçao. Voting to remain part of the Netherlands while its neighbors break away, the people of Bonaire maintain an unhurried pace, courting tourism but not becoming enraptured to the trappings that come with unbridled growth.

In the cultural stronghold of Rincon, fiestas celebrate the local pride and traditions. Coastal accommodations are built to favor the aesthetic, with few buildings over three storeys. The national park and flamingo nesting grounds cover perhaps a quarter of the island, giving the natural world

Dutch architecture dominates the island buildings

on land its due. The only concession to mass tourism may be the weekly visit of a cruise ship. But it will leave the same day, blasting its horn as the sun sets and leaving Bonaire to keep to itself.

This book will introduce you to the island's most revered resources – the coral reefs. It takes a look at remote northern shore dives in the Washington Slagbaai National Park, then makes a run down the coast looking at the combination of shore and boat dives that bring the diver into the lush world of dense corals and odd creatures like frogfish and seahorses. The turtle-nesting sanctuary at the offshore island of Klein Bonaire has stunning steep slopes and coral gardens with dive sites circling the island. The book also looks at the famous Bonaire pier dives, its famous *Hilma Hooker* shipwreck and the many shore dives opposite the island's saltpans in

the south. The guide also has a sampling of the 'wildside' – the windswept east coast that offers an opportunity to see a whole undersea world where few dare to go.

Bonaire probably has even more sites than are listed in this book. Plus, the unique wildlife, like its flamingoes and wild donkeys, make it a special place to spend some time. You will see why many divers come back year after year, enjoying the old familiar sites and discovering some new ones. It is truly a diver's paradise.

BONAIRE DIVE HIGHLIGHTS

1 **Boca Slagbaai** – a favorite of snorkelers and divers with some history and flamingoes thrown in.
2 **Karpata** – great undersea terrain with a good chance of seeing sea turtles and lots of other stuff.
3 **1000 Steps** – beautiful retreat for snorkelers and divers alike with a nice variety of marine life in a serene setting.
4 **Reef Scientifico** – this house reef in front of Captain Don's has a small shipwreck, big sponges and a resident barracuda.
5 **Town Pier** – colorful sponges and great macro make this a superb day and night dive.
6 **Jerry's Reef** – great place to see big sponges, black coral and other offerings of Klein Bonaire.
7 **Hilma Hooker** – signature dive for Bonaire wreckies, this ship is fun to explore and has good marine growth.
8 **Angel City** – explore the double reef here and see big eels and, yes, angelfish.
9 **Salt Pier** – a must-dive, this shallow maze is great for a long relaxed dive through shoals of fish.
10 **White Hole** – the best dive on the 'wildside' with schooling tarpon and pretty sea fans.

A pillar is smothered in sponge life at
Bonaire's famous Town Pier

Historic Rincon is the oldest village on Bonaire

Facts about Bonaire

OVERVIEW

Many destinations claim to be a diver's paradise. In Bonaire, it says so right on the license plate. Bonaire has made a commitment to preserve its reefs, which are its livelihood, but at the same time to forego true mass tourism in favor of a more controlled development of its economy.

If one looks at Bonaire's past, there has always been an air of independence and isolation. In the years after slavery was abolished, islanders were content to farm and ranch and pretty much keep to themselves.

It kind of slid into the world tourism scene and, rather reluctantly, it now embraces it. But it does this on its own terms, ensuring the health of its environment and natural resources take precedence over the temptation to sell out for the short term.

Bonaire, with 12,000 inhabitants, is part of the Netherlands Antilles. Together with Aruba and Curaçao it forms a group referred to as the ABC islands. But make no mistake, Bonaire, with a capital 'B', is its own entity and is happy to stay that way.

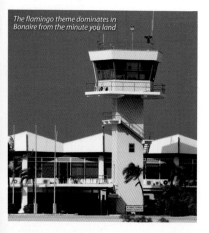

The flamingo theme dominates in Bonaire from the minute you land

HISTORY

Bonaire's history dates back at least 1000 years to the first inhabitants, the Caiquetios Indians, a part of the Arawak nation. There are indications the island may have had inhabitants as far back as 3000 years ago. Cave paintings from the Caiquetio habitation can be seen by following a turnoff on the road close to Rincon – it is marked by a sign. The Caiquetios came from coastal Venezuela and lived peacefully for five centuries until Europeans came to Bonaire in 1499. Alonso de Ojeda and Amerigo Vespucci claimed it for Spain. Unfortunately for the Caiquetios, the Spanish ruthlessly enslaved them and moved them off to work in plantations on the Island of Hispaniola, leaving the island unpopulated.

Bonaire's name is believed to be derived from these people. It comes from the Caiquetio word *'bonay'*, meaning 'low country'. The early Spanish and Dutch modified its spelling to Bojnaj and also Bonaire.

The island was sparsely settled until 1526. Cattle were brought to Bonaire by the governor and Caiquetios were returned to become agricultural workers. The island became a center for raising sheep, goats, pigs, horses and donkeys. They were raised for their skins, not their meat, and roamed wild. Soon, large herds of animals greatly outnumbered the people. Wild donkeys and goats still inhabit the *kunuku* (outback). However, due to a number of car accidents most donkeys are found at the Donkey Sanctuary. The goats still roam.

Bonaire's early inhabitants were mostly convicts from Spanish colonies in South America. The only permanent settlement was the village of Rincon. Situated in a valley far from a safe harbor, it was thought to be safe from

Divers leave for Klein Bonaire as a snorkeler watches

marauding pirates. In 1633, the Dutch took possession of Curaçao, Bonaire and Aruba. Curaçao, the largest island, became a slave trade center, while Bonaire became a plantation island of the Dutch West Indies Company. At that time the first African slaves were forced to work by cutting dyewood and cultivating maize and harvesting solar salt. The remnants of those sad days can be seen on the island's south coast, where there are small slave huts. The handmade salt-pans are still used today.

Until 1816, ownership of Bonaire changed hands a number of times, finally being returned that year to the Dutch as a result of the Treaty of Paris. By 1837, it was a thriving center of salt production. The abolition of slavery in 1863 brought an end to the human exploitation. The salt industry died and wasn't reborn again until the 1960s. Today it is a division of Cargill Incorporated, one of the world's largest salt producers.

Tourism was born when the government constructed the first pier for ships in the harbor. This allowed cruise ships to tie up and discharge passengers. It also made it easier to bring in goods and supplies for the island's residents. Hotels were built to house the early visitors. In 1943, the construction of a modern airport south of Kralendijk made it even easier for tourists to reach the island.

The island embraced scuba diving and nature over the past few decades, and has become one of the true international environmental success stories found in eco-travel. Bonaireans have learnt to balance their growth with the environment. Politically, they have chosen to remain aligned with the Netherlands as Aruba and Curaçao take another tack. The future holds some exciting new challenges for the island for growth and to cement its place in the region.

DIVING HISTORY

Total diving freedom is the mantra. In Bonaire, divers like to do what they want to do, any time and any place. They've been an independent lot since divers first came to the island and that attitude remains today. In the early days, divers went all over Bonaire by boat and by shore looking for dive sites. Pioneers include Bruce Bowker, Bas Marin, Nel Nicholas, Ebo Domacasse and Capt Don Stewart. Back then in the 1960s, one of the main scuba diving activities was spearfishing; harvesting from the sea was the norm. There were even international spearfishing competitions in Bonaire.

Capt Don (as he's known to the locals) recalls scuba divers weren't looked on fondly by others in the fledgling tourism industry in the 1960s. Divers wore their swimming suits everywhere and hauled gear around. But, rather than leave, they stayed and established their own hotels, bars and dive shops so they'd have places to hang out. This slowly but surely put Bonaire on the map as the diving destination of choice by divers all over the world.

Capt Don says he had an epiphany of sorts and felt spearfishing just wasn't a good thing. He vowed to be a shepherd of the sea and its resources. Others followed suit and through a friend named Carel Steensma (see the dive site **Carel's Vision**), Capt Don was able to approach Prince Bernhard of the Netherlands. He proposed the island be a marine preserve and the prince concurred. Since then, the Bonaire Marine Park has been a reality and Bonaire is regarded as one of the world's leaders in pioneering multiple use reef conservation.

A film documenting the captain's efforts, *Island Adrift* (also the name of his book) was filmed by Hendrik Wuyts and is available around Bonaire on DVD. Capt Don is also credited with finding and naming more than 50 dive sites,

personally placing mooring buoys at many of them. He is hailed by many as the founder of the dive industry on Bonaire, and an ardent conservationist. 'He helped give the island an identity. He helped give it a vision,' says George Buckley, professor of marine biology at Harvard.

Tourism has grown rapidly in the past two decades and is the island's main activity for visitors.

Today the management of the park is in the hands of Stichting Nationale Parken Bonaire, or STINAPA Bonaire. It manages the Bonaire National Marine Park, the Washington Slagbaai National Park, the caves at Barcadera, Klein Bonaire and three RAMSAR sites. RAMSAR sites are internationally recognized wetlands. It continues to fulfill the vision of the early pioneers and is recognized internationally as a model in marine park management.

The charismatic Capt Don is considered the diving pioneer of Bonaire

GEOGRAPHY

Bonaire is a small place and mostly volcanic. The island is 24 miles (38km) long and 3 to 7 miles (11km) at the widest point. It has 116 sq miles (300 sq km) of land, most of which is no good for agriculture, so the island is covered mainly in cactus and brush. It sits near Venezuela and has one small offshore island called Klein Bonaire, nestled in its western arch. Prevailing winds blow from the east all but about two months of the year (September and October) and the west side of Bonaire is protected by a central ridgeback. This leaves the water calm, making it the natural side to dive.

The north of Bonaire is mainly *kunukus* (big ranches) and a national park. In and near the park are numerous hills, the highest being Mount Brandaris at 723ft (241m). The south end is flat and almost at sea level, and made up of salt fields and a flamingo sanctuary.

The Netherlands Antilles has a tropical climate, with warm weather all year.

CLIMATE

Bonaire's tropical but pleasant climate is legendary. The average air temperature is 82° Fahrenheit (30ºC) and 75% relative humidity. For divers and snorkelers, the average water temperature is 80ºF (29ºC). Rainfall averages 22in (52.8cm) per year, mostly during the rainy season. There is a constant east trade wind that generally makes the evenings cool and comfortable. Average wind speed is 15mph (25kph).

The tourism high season is winter/spring: December 15 to April 14. The low season is summer/fall: April 15 to December 14. The stronger winds are May through August, with strong to moderate winds January through April. Calm season, when divers try to dive the east side, is September and October. Things green up for a few months in rainy season from November through January, although the rain usually comes at night or in bursts. It is rarely constant or torrential.

This lack of rainfall is good for divers as the water is normally clear with visibility averaging 100ft up to 150ft on a good day (30m to 45m).

POPULATION, PEOPLE & CULTURE

Bonaire's permanent residents are a friendly bunch with a rich history, steeped in the settling and commerce of the Caribbean. There are about 12,000 people on Bonaire. Many are Dutch citizens who have decided to give life in the tropics a try. The rest were born and raised here or on nearby islands.

Bonairean culture goes back many generations. This cultural history is evident in songs and dances traditionally seen during holidays and festivals. Nowadays, Catholicism is strong in the community and this has enforced strong family ties and respect for nature and an understanding of an environment.

The first settlers in this inhospitable, arid land were slaves and salt miners. Early days of slavery conditioned the people to be strong in the face of adversity. People began to develop songs, invent dances, and sing in the old African tradition. These songs and dances have now evolved into festivals that are an important part of Bonaire life and culture.

The dances of the Simidan and the Bari are the best known. The traditional waltz, mazurka and the polka and the local 'Baile di Sinta' (ribbon dance) are performed as well as the rumba, the carioca, and merengue that came from other islands. American jazz also influenced local traditions of song and dance. Using an eclectic assortment of homemade musical instruments, early performers set the stage for rich, local traditions.

The Samur is a unique vessel for a sunset sail

Thus, quite a few festivals occur throughout the year. The *Bonaire Reporter* or *Nights Magazine* alerts visitors to those taking place during their particular vacation period. The period from January 1 to 6 is Maskarada, which is worth seeing for the creative and colorful masks made in honor of this event. The Spring Harvest Festival occurs from the end of February until the end of April. Summer sees Dia di San Juan and Dia di San Pedro celebrations. Bari runs from the end of October to the end of December.

Many of the festivals are regional, even on small Bonaire. For instance, the main village of Rincon is more apt to celebrate all the holidays in grand style, while the village of North Salina devotes a lot of energy to Maskarada. The best example of strong cultural ties is during Dia Di Rincon (Rincon Day) when there are thousands of participants from the Antilles and Aruba that come to celebrate.

LANGUAGES

English is spoken almost everywhere, but there are many other major languages to hear. The official language of Bonaire is Dutch. But the native language is Papiamentu, spoken exclusively in the ABC Islands of Aruba, Bonaire, and Curaçao. Papiamentu is a mixture of many languages including Spanish, Dutch, Portuguese, French, English, Caribbean Indian and various African languages. An official spelling for Papiamentu words was established

The harbor holds some colorful boats and yachts

what's happening. Trans World Radio, an international Christian radio station with a big presence on Bonaire, also offers hourly English news (AM800).

Also, almost everyone here speaks Spanish. So if all else fails, one can usually converse in Spanish. Papiamentu language has strong Spanish roots and is close enough that one can make oneself understood when speaking Spanish.

GATEWAY CITY

Kralendijk

Divers have a Mecca – it is called Kralendijk. This colorful little city next to the Bonaire Flamingo Airport is the hub of the island, flanked on both sides by the island's major dive hotels. In town there are many fine restaurants, bars, gift shops, a visitor center, supermarkets and other support businesses that mainly revolve around tourist divers. The town square is a historic setting of an old Dutch fort and some older buildings still holding their own as part of a waterfront walkway and shopping district. Sailboats anchor in this protected setting and Klein Bonaire sits just across a channel where the sun sets with a warm afterglow most evenings. Many come to this area to shop and eat after a big day of diving and some also come to dive, as this is also the home of the famous **Town Pier**, one of the Caribbean's finest night dives.

several years ago, and dictionaries and language training materials can be found in the book stores.

All Antillean children are required to be fluent in Dutch as part of their schooling, so if you can speak Dutch, you'll be able to get around very well. There are a number of Dutch-language newspapers available on Bonaire and the pop music Mega FM radio station (FM101) features hourly news in Dutch during the workday.

English is also widely spoken and most of the fish guidebooks and other marine material are in English. There are local Dutch and Papiamentu language newspapers but no English language equivalent. The *Bonaire Reporter* is in English and has a touristy verve for those visiting and wanting to find out

Catholicism is the main religion here

Diving in Bonaire

Bonaire currently boasts over 355 species of fish as counted by experts and novices via REEF survey. It has healthy corals, clear water and plenty of dive sites. It is blessed as a diving destination and it wants to stay that way. Thus, it has established the entire marine ecosystem as a preserve and park. The nice thing about Bonaire, and somewhat unusual, is that virtually the whole population of 12,000 people has bought into the reef conservation philosophy that has been part of the island verve for a few decades now.

Can you say 'dive Nazi'? That's what many visitors may think when first confronted by all of the marine park rules and regulations. And Bonaire residents don't care. If you come here with a nonchalant attitude about the reefs and their inhabitants, they would rather you take your money, dive gear and attitude elsewhere. This somewhat militant but refreshing attitude of 'fish first' sets the island apart from just about every other dive destination in the world.

Bonaire established the first national park in the Caribbean in 1969 and the first marine park 10 years later. Now, Bonaire Marine Park is the island body charged with governing the use of the waters surrounding Bonaire in order to protect its marine life. The Marine Park extends from the high water mark to the 200ft (60m) depth contour, encompassing the entire coast of Bonaire and Klein Bonaire – an area of about 2700 hectares, including coral reef, seagrass, and mangroves.

Bonaire Marine Park is a model of its kind in the Caribbean (and the world for that matter), protecting the marine environment in its care while maximizing safe levels of use for recreation and commerce. It maintains more than 100 public moorings, conducts extensive scientific research, provides informa-

Iguanas are ubiquitous on the island

tion to users and monitors human and natural impacts.

Recognized worldwide as an exemplary marine park, it has eliminated destructive fishing practices and discharge of polluted ballast water. It has also banned spearfishing, collecting of corals, shells, and other marine life, and use of anchors.

Every diver and snorkeler must first go through an orientation covering the park's rules. These are conducted by dive masters at the dive shops before a newly arrived diver is allowed to start diving. Divers are also asked to do a shore checkout dive to get weight right so improper buoyancy doesn't cause a diver to crash into the reef on boat dives.

Admission fees are the sole dependable income of the park. Whether you are a diver, snorkeler, fisherman, yachtsman or windsurfer, if you use the water, you must purchase an admission tag. Tags are available at dive shops, windsurf centers and the Marine Park headquarters at Barcadera. Cost is $10 for snorkelers and $25 for divers. The tags are good for a full year so divers going to Bonaire twice in a year don't have to pay again unless they want to.

A snorkeler watches divers enter the water at 18th Palm

The park provides some very informative literature at dive shops, hotels and all park outlets including BNMP brochures on *Boating Regulations, Clean up Dives, Cruising Bonaire, Diving Bonaire, Fishing Regulations, Marine Park Fees, Protected Species, Snorkeling* and *Underwater Photography & Video.*

The sites in this book are following the BNMP's latest official mooring site numbers and names for the most part, with the exception of a couple of sites on the east side. The newest open and closed sites were included at the time the book was written.

WHAT TO BRING

The climate in Bonaire is best described as arid but still tropical. The east coast is largely undeveloped and Bonaire is blessed with a fairly continuous breeze 10 months of the year. This normally keeps things pleasant across the island. The winds usually die down in September and October but then start back in November. Along the east coast where divers visit, this means there is usually a soft wind blowing out to sea, keeping the west coast calm and tranquil year round. This is one of Bonaire's major reasons for being such a great dive destination.

So, if you're staying on the east coast, you may want a light jacket or sweater at night. Long-sleeved T-shirts or cotton shirts or blouses are also helpful. It can also be cool at water's edge in the evenings, so a jacket or long garment. Many divers like to night dive, so a fleece parka or something warm after the dive is a smart idea. Evening clothes are casual to casual-nice, depending on your hotel or restaurant.

Bring light clothing. No one wears suits for anything day or night. Shorts, T-shirts, swimwear and sandals or flip-flops get you by almost anywhere. For beachside hikes (there are nice walking paths) and exploring the hills and

Best Dives

Wreck Dive

The **Hilma Hooker** is one of the most attractive dives in the Caribbean with resident tarpon and good sponge growth. At night the tubastrea corals blossom.

Reef Dive

Karpata is considered one of the best dives on the island and its combination of corals and fish, shallow and deep, makes it stand above the rest.

Town Pier's blossoming tube corals

Hard corals on the upper reef

Critter Dive

With a documented count of 317 fish species, you can see just about anything you want at **Bari's Reef**. And the invertebrates are plentiful too.

Shark Dive

The best chance to see a shark may be at the hard-to-get-to **Spelonk** on the east side. But the combination of wall, waves, wrecks and a few sharks make this a wild dive.

Pier Dive

Town Pier has to be one of the best dives anywhere, with its colorful sponge growth and encrusting invertebrate life. At night, the small stuff comes out. And it's shallow!

Marine Park Rules (some, not all)

1 Every diver must have a valid diving tag and attach it to their BC. These can be purchased from all dive operators.
2 A dive orientation from a valid dive operator is mandatory before anyone can dive in BNMP.
3 Anchoring is forbidden. Mooring buoys must be used.
4 Spearfishing is prohibited. Spear guns must be left at the customs office.
5 It is forbidden to remove anything alive or dead from the BNMP.
6 Do not damage the reefs in any way. Don't touch the corals and avoid sitting on the bottom.

national park, bring some sturdy hiking or running shoes. Also, bring a hat and sunglasses to protect from the sun.

Bring a good sunscreen for daytime sun protection. At dusk and at night you'll want some insect repellent. 'No-see-ums' and mosquitoes can be a bother and are a fact of life, especially during the rainy months of November through January.

Topless sunbathing and nudity is prohibited on beaches except for Sorobon Beach Resort (a privately owned nudist resort). But topless sunbathing is seen at some of the hotels with a more European clientele.

WHAT TO BRING DIVING

Bonaire is a good place for a dive trip because if you do forget something, there are many fully-equipped dive shops on the island that offer both rental and sales. If you're not picky and don't want to carry dive gear, full rental of all kit is also available.

The water is tropical and clear. Temperature is generally 78-84°F (25.6-28.9°C), so all that is needed is a 1.5mm to 3mm wetsuit to remain very comfortable. Heartier folks just wear skins or T-shirts. Those acclimated, like

About Shore Diving

Several factors combine to offer Bonaire visitors shore diving opportunities unlike any found elsewhere in the Caribbean.

One is the sheer number of shore dive sites available. With over 50 marked sites, and any number of easily accessible unmarked entry points to choose from, divers will run out of vacation time long before they run out of diving options.

Bonaire's calm west coast waters make entering the water for your dive safe and easy. And with a fringing reef no more than 50 yards off shore, surface swims are kept to a minimum. Freedom-loving divers are sure to enjoy the unlimited shore diving packages that some dive centers offer.

The one downside is that break-ins and theft from unguarded vehicles parked at dive sites is rampant, especially for night divers. The local advice is leave nothing of value in your vehicle and leave the vehicle open and unlocked. Also, don't try to hide something in the bushes or nearby. The obvious places are usually scouted and relieved of their treasures as well.

A guide aids a diver exiting the sea

Rating System for Dives & Divers

Healthy corals are one of Bonaire's main attractions

The dive sites in this book are rated according to the following system. These are not absolute ratings but apply to divers at a particular time, diving at a particular place. For instance, someone unfamiliar with prevailing conditions might be considered a novice diver at one dive area, and an intermediate diver at another, more familiar location.

Novice:
A novice diver generally fits the following profile:
- basic scuba certification from an internationally recognized certifying agency
- dives infrequently (less than one trip a year)
- logged fewer than 25 total dives
- little or no experience diving in similar waters and conditions
- dives no deeper than 60ft (18m).

*An instructor or divemaster should accompany a novice diver on all dives.

Intermediate:
An intermediate diver generally fits the following profile:
- may have participated in some form of continuing diver education
- logged between 25 and 100 dives
- no deeper than 130ft (40m)
- has been diving in similar waters and conditions within the last six months.

Advanced:
An advanced diver generally fits the following profile:
- advanced certification
- has been diving for more than two years; logged over 100 dives
- has been diving in similar waters and conditions within the last six months.

Pre-Dive Safety Guidelines
Regardless of skill level, you should be in good physical condition and know your limitations. If you are uncertain as to which category you fit, ask the advice of a local dive instructor. He or she is best qualified to assess your abilities based on the prevailing dive conditions at any given site. Ultimately you must decide if you are capable of making a particular dive, depending on your level of training, recent experience, and physical condition, as well as water conditions at the site. Remember water conditions can change at any time, even during a dive.

divemasters, wear 5mm to 7mm. But tourists should be fine in the 1.5mm to 3mm range.

Otherwise, normal scuba gear or snorkeling gear is fine for Bonaire. Bonaire has many outlets for equipment sales, parts purchase like a fin strap and even repair. Shore diving is a big deal in Bonaire and sometimes the only way to see certain sites. Make sure you have good booties for coming in and out of the water across a reef or rocky beach.

Do NOT bring a spear gun. They are illegal and you will have to surrender it to customs or police until you leave. If you try to use one and are caught (highly likely), the fines are stiff and you will probably have to leave Bonaire. Bring a camera instead.

There are also tight restrictions on the use of gloves, although they can be stowed in pockets and used to go up and down the mooring line. Gloves can also be used during clean up dives, while wreck diving and to get into and out of the water when shore diving the windward side east of **Willemstoren**. Otherwise, if you have a medical reason for needing to wear gloves, please contact the Marine Park. If not: no gloves.

Nitrox is offered almost everywhere. Don't forget your C-card and dive log to show your host dive shop. And bring your mixed gas card if you are going to use Nitrox. Rebreather diving, rental and training are also available on Bonaire.

Looking down at 1000 Steps' Beach

DIVE TRAINING & CERTIFICATION

Bonaire offers all levels of training from snorkeling and basic scuba to full instructor courses. PADI is the main agency represented on the island. TDI technical diving courses are also offered. Check with your dive shop to see what courses you can take. Bonaire is perfect for Nitrox, wreck certification, marine life courses and many other specialties.

Most costs for diving are pretty much the same across the island. It is best to shop for what you want. Remember, the cheapest package may or may not be the best and safest training. Ask questions and shop for the best situation for your needs.

All levels of instruction are found, like this session at Captain Don's pool

Photographing sponges at Town Pier

DIVE OPERATORS

Most of Bonaire's hotels have an affiliated dive shop. Bonaire has an organization that most dive shops belong to. The Council of Underwater Resort Operators (CURO) has its members participate in establishing standards and uniform practices that, along with the Bonaire Marine Park Rules, work to preserve the reefs and the fragile ecosystem. These standards are tourist friendly, so a CURO member is a good bet.

There are also independents that offer private guiding and instruction services. Since there is so much shore diving, private guides are in demand and some are extremely good. Most rely on word of mouth and reputation,

Snorkeling near Andrea II

so ask fellow divers about those offering private guide services.

Others, like Dee Scarr of Touch the Sea, offer a naturalist experience as one-on-one and very small group interaction. Scarr is a longtime Bonaire environmentalist and experienced naturalist whose goal is to help divers and snorkelers better understand marine creatures. Another is Sea & Discover. Run by Caren Eckrich, a marine biologist and PADI dive instructor, she teaches people about the reefs through fun and interactive snorkel and dive programs. She is best known for her kids' program, Reef Explorers, where children learn about ocean creatures and ecosystems, improve their water skills and become one with the sea.

The Divi Flamingo Beach Resort specializes in scuba diving for the disabled. Some guest rooms and all common areas and dive shops are wheelchair accessible.

See the listing at the back of the book for approved dive operators and guide services.

Snorkeling is very popular on Bonaire

LIVE ABOARDS

There are currently no live aboards operating around Bonaire.

SNORKELING

As the water here is very clear, shore access is easy and the currents are normally mild, snorkeling is a very popular pastime. Many people come to Bonaire for the snorkeling alone. Klein Bonaire is a popular snorkeling spot. Kayakers often paddle to a spot and snorkel. And walk-ins at the popular beaches are a daily occurrence. Experienced snorkelers love to night snorkel on Bonaire.

It is necessary for all who use the waters of the Bonaire National Marine Park to pay a Nature Fee of $10 per year ($25 for scuba divers), and this includes snorkelers. Like divers, snorkelers receive a designated tag. The tag allows complimentary admission to Washington-Slagbaai National park, which has some nice beaches and great flamingo viewing.

Tags are available at all dive operations, hotels, resorts, windsurfing operations, sport fishing charter boats, sail/snorkel/water taxi operations, marinas, and other water sports operations on Bonaire.

The island's west-central coast

Beautiful tube sponges at Town Pier

UNDERWATER PHOTOGRAPHY

Underwater photography is a favorite pastime of many divers coming to Bonaire. The brilliant orange elephant ear sponges and bright purple tube sponges, gorgonian sea fans, Christmas tree worms and beautiful reef fish make Bonaire a great place for colorful wide-angle lens work, medium focal length for fish and macro photos.

Most of the larger dive centers have a staff pro who can provide instruction, camera rental or shoot personal video. E-6 film processing is becoming harder to find as digital is taking over the photo scene in leaps and bounds. Ask if your dive center offers it before you go if you want on-the-spot results.

Most dive centers have personal video services and there are companies like Scuba Vision that also join the boats of dive centers and offer a video at a reasonable fee.

Going on boat dives and especially shore dives with a good Bonaire underwater photographer is highly recommended. The longtime guides all know one another. If seahorses are seen at **Witches Hut**, the better guides will know where to look for them. You may hear a rumor that the seahorses are at **Andrea II** and look all day and find nothing. A good guide will be in the know about where the good critters are and where they can be found, making your photo experience much better in the long run.

ging yours as well. This can cause latches to unlock and uncovered domes and ports to get scratched. While it seems like a good idea to keep your camera wet all the time, the lack of enough boat basins and the overcrowding at the shop can be a problem. Better to keep your camera wet with a damp towel on board and then soak it in the room bathtub until they get a handle on camera care.

Also, be warned that the sand here is very fine at most beaches. Since beach diving is a major part of the dive scene, entries in and out of surf zones where there is a lot of fine sand in the water can be harmful to the health of your camera. After beach dives, carefully check and clean your O-rings to ensure fine sand particles have not got lodged in the O-ring slots and on the rings themselves. A little preventive maintenance in the evenings can save many dollars in replacing a camera due to a housing flooded because of an errant speck of beach sand.

Goatfish along the upper reef

In Bonaire, you will find that underwater photography is catered to, but not in a huge way. Most boats have fresh water buckets that can hold perhaps three housed point-and-shoot cameras and strobes (or one SLR system). On land, the tanks dedicated to camera rinse can be rather crowded, with both boat and shore divers sharing the same bin, and masks and fins allowed to be washed in the same water. In doing this book, we found few operations that actually had large specific dedicated camera-only rinse tanks, and those that did had only one and those weren't exactly large.

We point this out as most divers use wrist lanyards, and a crowded rinse bin and boat rinse tub can mean people hastily pulling their gear out and snag-

Conservation

This island is a conservationist's Mecca. Plants, animals and marine life all get a lot of attention from various groups here. STINAPA (Stichting Nationale Parken) is the umbrella organization overseeing most environmental concerns. There is also a local sea turtle foundation. Scientists and researchers have come here for years for various marine related projects. STINAPA is the lead organization for most local and regional conservation efforts. Capt Don Stewart also started the Accolades program to honor those who have given personal time to aid Bonaire's environment and also to people worldwide involved in saving the sea and earth.

Every diver must buy a marine park use tag

Accolade Foundation

The Accolade Foundation recognizes individuals all over the world for their efforts to protect, manage and educate about environments. These people have inspired others to get involved and to do something to protect and educate about nature. A brainchild of Capt Don Stewart, the folks nominated for an Accolade are those who put their personal time and effort into making the marine world better for everyone.

Here is part of the philosophy of the unique, Bonaire-based Accolade Foundation:

- We all need to better understand nature, its myriad forms of life and their interactions. Collectively, recipients of the Accolade have had a wide impact on people young and old. The Foundation aims to spread the word about their efforts so as to recognize what they have accomplished and inspire others to follow the paths they have illuminated
- The effort needed to save planet earth from environmental degradation is a Herculean task. While individuals can and do have significant success with environmental issues, collectively they can be a force majeure whose power will be acknowledged locally, nationally and internationally. The Accolade Foundation hopes to be the spark that ignites worldwide collaborative effort to promote sound environmental management practices
- The power of one individual multiplied by thousands of others can and must be heard from mountains and valleys and across oceans; from villages and cities to the leaders of all governments. Then and only then will begin the healing process to stop environmental degradation
- With the technological and electronic wonders of today, for once we have the power to communicate instantly across the globe. Let us start the conversation. Let the small clapping of hands from Bonaire (considering Bonaire is to coral reef preservation what Greenwich is to time) resonate to the thunderous wave of activism around the world.

Protected Species

Young hawksbill sea turtle

Animal and plant species found on Bonaire and Klein Bonaire that are globally threatened and in danger of extinction include:

- **Corals and marine life:** all types of soft and hard coral and sea fans, dead and alive, are locally and internationally protected by law. Coral reefs rival rain forests in their biological diversity. The magnificent array of reef fish and bottom-dwelling animals, such as crustaceans, that visitors enjoy observing all depend on the health of the coral reef. In addition, the coral reefs provide food and income for the Bonairean people. The black corals, which have been heavily exploited in some Caribbean countries, are completely protected on Bonaire, as are all other corals. Black coral used in jewelry is the internal skeletal structure of the living coral, and grows very slowly. For many species of coral, one inch of growth may take decades
- **Marine mammals:** mammals, such as whales, porpoises and dolphins, are fully protected locally and internationally
- **Birds:** Bonaire is home to diverse bird populations, all of which are protected. Flamingos, loras and parakeets are also protected under CITES (Convention on International Trade in Endangered Species). The lora, the island's local parrot, isn't found anywhere else in the world. Bonaire is also home to one of only four surviving breeding colonies in the world of southern flamingos. It is illegal to buy, possess or receive products containing their feathers
- **Lizards, iguanas and bats**: benefit from local and internationally protection
- **Plants:** all plants are protected by domestic law, and many, including orchids, lilies, cacti, bromeliads, and lignum vitae trees, are CITES regulated. Bonaire once was forested with hardwoods, including the slow-growing *lignum vitae* (tree of life). Coveted as a wood for shipbuilding, you see the tree only rarely now. Let us protect what is left. Orchids are rare due to the dry climate, but occupy an important niche in the ecosystem. Cacti are a key element in soil conservation. You may see some small bromeliads, also known as air ferns – don't disturb them
- **Sea turtles:** completely protected as are their nests and eggs, by both local and international law as they are threatened worldwide by overexploitation. It is illegal to catch, kill, eat, possess, offer for sale, sell, buy, trade or give as a gift turtle meat or any other part of a turtle. Bonaire and Klein Bonaire are nesting grounds for four species of sea turtle.

Courtesy STINAPA

Health & Safety

Overall, Bonaire is a healthy place to visit. There are no exotic diseases and the mosquito bites only lead to itching. The island has a 60-bed hospital; Hospital San Francisco at Kaya Soeur Bartola #2 in Kralendijk. There are a number of doctors practicing on the island. There is an ambulance plane on call for emergencies. The emergency phone number for the hospital ambulance is ☎ 114.

The pharmacy, in downtown Kralendijk, Botica Bonaire, is well stocked and the pharmacists seem to be quite familiar with diving maladies like sore ears and coral cuts.

PRE-TRIP PREPARATION

There are a number of shops in Bonaire that offer equipment for sale and rental and there is some equipment repair available as well. But if you own your own gear you will want to get your regulator tuned up before coming here, if you haven't used it for six months or so. You may also want to do some local 'check out' dives, even if just in a pool, to check things out.

Also, get some exercise prior to the trip so you can face the challenges of boat diving and more so, the ins and outs and walks associated with shore diving. Swimming, hiking with a backpack and jogging will help increase fitness and stamina.

Make sure your passport is not about to expire or hasn't already expired. You can't get into Bonaire without one and you can't get back home even if you do manage to get into Bonaire.

MEDICAL & RECOMPRESSION FACILITIES

A hyperbaric recompression chamber is located adjacent to the hospital and is run by highly trained staff and aided by a number of dive professionals working on the island. To be admitted, one must go via the emergency room at the hospital. The emergency phone number for the ambulance is ☎ 114. Your DAN affiliate should also be consulted in the event of a diving accident or diving illness symptoms, as well as your dive shop manager, so they can react to the emergency and set things in motion for treatment.

DAN

Divers Alert Network (DAN) is an international membership association of individuals and organizations sharing a common interest in diving and safety. It operates a 24-hour diving emergency hotline in the US at ☎ 919-684-8111 or ☎ 919-684-4DAN (which accepts collect calls in a dive emergency). DAN does not directly provide medical care; however, it does provide advice on early treatment, evacuation, and hyperbaric treatment of diving-related injuries.

In-water instruction near Town Pier

A flamingo tongue shell clings to a fan coral

Washington Slagbaai National Park

Schooling doctorfish swim over the upper reef

This park is a cactus wonderland. Lizards and iguanas warming themselves on the road scurry from the slow approach of your vehicle. Unlike the developed part of the island, the park has rolling hills, small lakes, bays and forests of brush and cactus, thinned somewhat by wild goats and a dwindling population of wild donkeys. Birds of prey sit in twisted trees, while elegant pink flamingoes wade through the shallows of broad saltwater estuaries foraging for food.

PARK DIVING

BNMP's (Bonaire National Marine Park's) numbered dive sites start at Number 1 – **Boka Bartol** on the northwest corner of Bonaire – and run south to the island's southern tip, with a few more park sites extending back up the east coast to the Lac.

Wild and remote, the beauty and solitude that comes from isolation is also a factor to be considered when diving in Washington Slagbaai.

The roads are scheduled to be paved in some places in the park, but for the most part they are one-way single lanes little more than dirt tracks. If you should have any sort of diving accident, whether it be slipping and breaking a bone or a hyperbaric emergency, it is a good hour from the closest park dive site to any medical treatment. So shallower dives and favorable entry conditions are the best and safest way to approach diving here.

There are seven sites within the park and all but one (at this writing) are open to the diving community by shore. The diving here is considered to be more virgin, as dive boats and shore divers don't get up here as frequently. If you are boat diving, many dive operations will spend two dives up in the park waters as it is considered a long way to go for a dive, and will therefore maximize the experience.

Washington Slagbaai National Park	GOOD SNORKELING	NOVICE	INTERMEDIATE	ADVANCED
1 BOKA BARTOL	•			•
2 PLAYA BENGE	•			•
3 PLAYA FUNCHI	•	•		
4 BISE MORTO	•	•		
5 WAYAKA	•	•		
6a BOKA SLAGBAAI NORTH	•	•		
6b BOKA SLAGBAAI SOUTH	•	•		

Blowholes and rugged cliffs are found in the National Park's boundaries

1   BOKA BARTOL

Location: *Washington Slagbaai National Park*
Depth: *15-85ft (4-27m)*
Access: *Shore or boat*
Expertise Rating: *Advanced and/or with guide*

This broad and beautiful bay is a favorite dive and snorkel site for park visitors. The sandy inner reef area studded with corals and small channels is a snorkeler's delight. Since it sits at the northern tip of Bonaire it is wise to evaluate conditions before entering the water here.

As with most of the park sites, it is not as protected as those further south, and careful attention should be paid to surf and weather conditions here. Stronger currents usually accompany a big surf, so even if you get out, you may run into current problems. Since no-one lives up here, it is necessary to drive up and check the seas. Do not be afraid to abort a dive or snorkel if conditions aren't favorable. Even though it is a long drive, better safe than sorry.

If entering by shore, park at the south end of the boka and make your way down the small beach area at the shore. If snorkeling, enjoy the many corals and sandy areas in this boka, and keep an eye out for big barracuda coasting by. The STINAPA buoy sits offshore in 27ft of water, the block base being in a sandy area that basically marks the beginning of the sloping reef. If diving, head out through one of the shallow channels and admire the shallow corals on the way out. Drop down at the buoy and you will see there is a sandy area that again turns into slope and more corals and channels.

The best diving is about 30ft to 80ft. Since this area isn't dived or fished heavily, parrotfish, grouper and many other species can be larger here and more abundant. The sand channels hold a multitude of garden eels at around 50ft to 60ft and further down. Look also for stingrays buried in the white sand.

On the way up, check out the odd coral formations and make your deco stop, enjoying the many shallow corals. This shallow area can get quite stirred up when there is strong surf and visibility can be low on exit, which is another reason to carefully consider this dive if it isn't a nice day.

Also, when diving, look into the blue water. The park's first few dive sites have been places where eagle rays, turtles, the occasional manta and even a whale shark have been seen.

2 PLAYA BENGE

Location: *Washington Slagbaai National Park*
Depth: *10-140ft (3-35m)*
Access: *Shore or boat*
Expertise Rating: *Advanced and/or with guide*

This is another of the trickier dives in the park. Conditions need to be evaluated here carefully for both divers and snorkelers. Wind-driven waves can cause the inner-reef area to fill quickly, and the only means for water to escape is the center channel where divers and snorkelers like to enter. Thus, it can be a rip of a ride out and a real struggle to get back in the same way. Don't dive or snorkel if the strong wind is coming into your face as you look out onto the reef.

Although we have the wall icon listed, it is not a true wall, but rather quite a steep slope. On the right, the coral is in heavy concentration, with the south being sand and coral heads. Deep dives can be made past the buoy's base

A hawksbill sea turtle wings in from the blue

from 30ft down to 110ft. Here a deep lip starts and holds pocked areas and a small cave. One cavern is actually a swim-through.

Big fish abound here and this is also a good place to keep an eye out for pelagics. The basin-shape of the wall area sweeps currents over the corals but also protects them. Thus, they are competitive and healthy here. Star, brain and other hard corals compete for space.

This white sandy beach is also a nesting area for sea turtles, so watch your step when crossing the beach so as not to disturb the nests. Again, evaluate conditions before entering.

The beach and nearby saliña make
Playa Funchi a scenic site

| 3 | **PLAYA FUNCHI** |

Location: *Washington Slagbaai
National Park*
Depth: *15-90ft (4-28m)*
Access: *Shore or boat*
Expertise Rating: *Novice*

Funchi, or a traditional corn meal mush, is an Antillean staple. Since the beach is full of coral rubble, it isn't mushy at all. Local folks like to eat it with fish, so maybe the reef reminded someone of fish and funchi. They also eat it sliced and fried in butter and served with crisp bacon and scrambled eggs for Sunday breakfast. Maybe the beach was a good place to spend Sunday morning. No matter how it got its name, it is a nice place for snorkelers and divers. The reef has lots of nooks and crannies in the coral and marine invertebrates are in good numbers here.

The buoy here sits in 28ft of water but it is not on the drop-off. A swim of a couple minutes brings the diver out to the slope. Look for marauding jacks along the reef and also schooling jacks. Again, this area has larger fish down deep than are seen further south.

The reef slope has coral cover from about 30ft to 100ft and then becomes a sand plain. There are some nice sponge formations here and small cleaning areas with barber pole shrimp and hiding eels.

Since it is a three to four minute swim once back up at the 30ft mark, give yourself plenty of time and air to get back into the shallows.

Snorkelers feed the fish here – although they're asked not to – so angels and others may seem overly friendly. They're just looking for a handout. Fish feeding is against BNMP regulations everywhere, by the way, which is why there aren't 'pet' morays and other such creatures found at other Caribbean destinations.

4 BISE MORTO

Location: *Washington Slagbaai National Park*
Depth: *20-100ft (6-30m)*
Access: *Closed*
Expertise Rating: *Novice*

This site is closed for a while. The park authority occasionally closes some areas on land and sea so they can be relieved of visitor and diver pressure. This can be a long time or a short time. The park puts no real deadline on opening and closing a site. They just monitor these closed sites to see how they are doing, so ask if you hear a place is closed, as it might re-open. Also, don't be surprised to find a site closed, but normally they only close one or two of the island's many areas at a time.

Bise Morto has a small beach and a buoy in 25ft of water. It has a long sandy inner reef plain that eventually slopes and runs down to about 120ft to 130ft and turns again to sand. Hard corals abound.

A spotted moray is a commonly seen eel

Hurricane Lenny

Mid-November 1999 is a time that Bonaire residents recall with trepidation. A tropical depression started building on November 13, and in a short time Tropical Depression number 16 evolved into the eighth hurricane of the season, dubbed Lenny. Hurricanes at this time of the year are a rare occurrence. Not only was Lenny remarkably intense for a late-season hurricane, but the system also made a nearly unprecedented eastward track through the Caribbean Sea. Only four other hurricanes reached category 3 or greater on the Saffir-Simpson Scale. Lenny was a strong category 4 when it tracked past Puerto Rico and the US Virgin Islands. During this century, only three other hurricanes moved pre-dominantly east or northeastward through the Caribbean at any time of the year; in 1905, 1939 and 1955 (all in October). Most of the late season tropical systems that form over the Caribbean move northward.

The storm did not actually hit Bonaire, but the swell from the intense storm rolled into the north and western coast and wreaked havoc on the normally tranquil coast. Bonaire was known for its coral growth that came right up to the shoreline in many places. Capt Don tells tales of having to actually hack paths through the coral just to get out to shore dive. The powerful waves wiped out a lot of coral in the shallows and down to 30ft in some places. Coastal erosion was rampant and many homes, businesses and piers were destroyed.

Bonaire buffs still reflect on the rich reefs before Lenny. However, corals are now rebounding and regrowing along the western reefs, while fish have new habitats and the change in the reef structure has opened up the coastal areas for different invertebrate species and fish to move in.

Anyone who had not been to Bonaire before would not be able to see much of the damage, unless it was pointed out. It is good to know how nature builds and then changes the ocean floor. This is evident in Bonaire and the reefs are rebounding well, making for a rewarding diving experience.

The short set of steps leads to Wayaka's entry

5 WAYAKA

Location: *Washington Slagbaai National Park*
Depth: *15-130ft (4-40m)*
Access: *Shore and boat*
Expertise Rating: *Novice*

This is also a dive and snorkel site with the park buoy in fairly shallow water at 21ft. Snorkelers are very partial to this site. There is a small sandy beach that all but disappears at high tide, and this site also has a *saliña* nearby that flamingoes like to frequent. To get to the beach you have to go down a set of a dozen steps with a handrail. This leads to the beach area and there are a number of entries along the shoreline. The sand is very fine and there are rocks as you get deeper.

This is a long swim out for snorkelers and divers also have to swim along the bottom to get to the drop-off if heading to the reef from the buoy line. Once out through the shallow channel and out to sea or off the boat, the reef makes a gentle decline down to a depth of 130ft. Look in the depths for the fernlike black coral. Not many Caribbean islands still have this type of coral, due to its use as jewelry and other hand-carved items.

This is a good place for midnight parrotfish, rays and turtles. Move back up the reef slowly to enjoy the variety here. Coral heads vary in size, giving this site a nice topography and a lot of places for the divers to look around.

A gray angel is a curious photo subject

Historic buildings are found at Boka Slagbaai

6a BOKA SLAGBAAI NORTH

Location: *Washington Slagbaai National Park*
Depth: *17-120ft (5-35m)*
Access: *Shore and boat*
Expertise Rating: *Novice*

This is a popular site for both diving and snorkelling. The area is seen easily from **Wayaka**. There is a scenic old harbor and historic buildings that have been renovated and can be visited by those coming here. There is even a picnic area and a *saliña* nearby that normally has flamingoes. Kayakers also come here to explore. The original buildings date back to 1868.

The beach is rubbly with sandy pockets in many places. Entry is pretty easy in most spots but on the north, there is a sandy beach at the start of the inlet and this is a good place to get in as there is less wave action when the swell comes from the north. The bottom has very few obstacles as you fin up and head out.

There are two BNMP buoys here, and both sit in 17ft of water at each end of the bay. Swim out and descend. Take note of the current and its strength. The currents here are not usually strong but there is usually some current.

The reef starts in 30ft to 35ft and slopes down to sand at 115ft to 125ft. Hard corals are in abundance, as well as

sponge life and big fish. Big green morays are found here. Look for shoals of Creole wrasse, French and queen angelfish and hawksbill turtles. If you're lucky, manta may appear in the blue.

6b BOKA SLAGBAAI SOUTH

Location: *Washington Slagbaai National Park*
Depth: *17-120ft (5-35m)*
Access: *Shore and boat*
Expertise Rating: *Novice*

On the other side of the old harbor and historic buildings is another parking area and open access to the shore. The slaagbai to the east can be seen easily here and so can the wildlife, so look for flamingoes and other water fowl. Slagbaai is a natural bay. This commonly used word for a brackish, shallow bay actually comes from the Dutch word *slachtbaai* (slaughters bay). From the 1860s, the Dutch shipped slaughtered and salted goats to Curaçao from here, and also began to transport salt. The old buildings represent the office, several stores, a slaughterhouse and a house of a superintendent from those days. The buildings can now be reserved for family or company gatherings and picnics.

Entry to this site is also easy as there is more beach area at this end of the cove. Again, take the long swim out past the buoy. Look for turtles, big parrotfish, lobsters and some blue water creatures when diving here. The tube sponges here are pink and purple and there are large barrel sponges. There are some nice translucent vase sponges as well.

Take care not to snorkel or come back too close to the bay's cliff line if there is a swell as you may get tossed around from the backwash. This is a great place to spend a day, and not all that far from the park's exit.

West Coast North Dive Sites

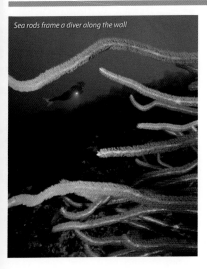
Sea rods frame a diver along the wall

West Coast North Dive Sites	GOOD SNORKELING	NOVICE	INTERMEDIATE	ADVANCED
7 NUKOVE	•	•		
8 CAREL'S VISION	•	•		
9 KARPATA	•		•	
10 LA DANIA'S LEAP	•		•	
11 RAPPEL			•	
12 BLOODLET			•	
13 TOLO / OL' BLUE	•	•		
14 COUNTRY GARDEN	•	•		
15 BON BINI NA KAS	•	•		
16 1000 STEPS	•		•	
17 WEBER'S JOY / WITCHES HUT	•	•		
18 JEFF DAVIS MEMORIAL	•	•		
19 KALLIS REEF	•	•		
20 OIL SLICK LEAP	•	•		
21 BARCADERA		•		
22 ANDREA II	•	•		
23 ANDREA I	•	•		

The area of former *kunukus* along the island's northwest coast, below the park boundaries and stretching down into Kralendijk, are what Bonaire dive guides call the north dive sites, no matter how they actually face. The sites past the airport are called south, no matter how they actually sit on the compass.

These are some of the most popular and heavily dived sites in Bonaire. They are just a short drive from the northern hotel row along mostly undeveloped coastline (although that is rapidly changing), and they offer a good variety of terrain, from broad, sandy beaches to rocky cliffs where you leap into the sea. Underwater terrain varies from quick drop-offs to gently sloping coral-covered plains.

Fish and invertebrate variety here is good. Seahorses, frogfish, sea turtles, jawfish and lots of hard corals add to the usual suspects found along the Bonaire Reefs. This is a good area for photographers to grab a knowledgeable local guide to help out with spotting macro subjects and pointing out behavior.

7   NUKOVE

Location: *Northwest coast*
Depth: *24-140ft (7-37m)*
Access: *Boat*
Expertise Rating: *Novice*

Some say the most challenging part of diving here is finding the site. Then you have to clamber down some pretty rough 'steps' to a small beach. However, many divers like this site because it is often free of other divers.

Enter on the left as you face the beach. It is easy to see the sandy area that leads out to rocks and corals. Start a rather long swim out to the buoy. Go down to the mooring blocks and you will see the coral is healthy and recovering from any storm damage.

This is a nice sloping wall as it runs steep and has lots of hard corals, including black coral trees at the deeper reaches. Large, old growth corals are found here and big sponges abound. Very attractive topography fed by a current that keeps things big and healthy. Look for many cleaning stations in the 30ft to 70ft range on this reef.

8　CAREL'S VISION

Location: *Northwest Coast*
Depth: *20-130ft (4-40m)*
Access: *Boat*
Expertise Rating: *Novice*

This latest dive site was announced by Elsmarie Beukenboom, director of STINAPA (the organization that oversees both the Bonaire Marine Park and Washington-Slagbaai Park) in June 2005, while Philippe Cousteau was visiting the island.

Beukenboom, an active, lifelong conservationist on Bonaire, announced the naming of the site as Carel's Vision, located on the north end between **Oil Slick Leap** and BOPEC. The site is named after Carel Steensma, a principal mover and shaker on the island in helping to initiate and fund the marine park in its early years by bringing Capt Don and Prince Bernhard of the Netherlands together.

This is a good reef but still recovering, so there is some broken coral around from the 1999 storm wave damage. The upper reef margin is rubbly, but there are a lot of small fish and new corals taking hold.

Starting in about 25ft and sloping very steeply down below 100ft to sand, the reef has some black coral, lots of star corals, plate corals and a few good size brain corals.

Add to this big sponge and the opportunity to see something like a manta come in from the blue, and you have an interesting spot. The deep sand is a good place to look for southern stingrays.

There is nice hard coral here, plus French and queen angelfish, cruising bar jacks and grunts around the sparse sea plumes and other soft corals up shallow.

This site has one of the newer drilled eyelets for the mooring buoys that do

The Windjammer

In between the park's southwest border and the sites that move south from **Karpata** is BOPEC, an international terminal where oil freighters dock to unload oil for the island's power and petrol resources. This area has recently been placed out of bounds due to international security regulations stemming from the international war on terror.

This announcement is somewhat of a disappointment to divers, especially deep diving techies, as the wreck of the *Windjammer* is sitting in the security area in deep water. It is a historic three-masted iron cargo ship. Originally called the *Mairi Bhan* (Scottish Gaelic for Bonnie Mary), built in 1874 in Scotland. She was carrying a cargo of asphalt, and wrecked off Bonaire in December 1912. Divers made the effort to dive her as she was in remarkably good shape and could be entered. Divers could swim inside the steel rib structure of the ship.

Recent reports say she has finally shown some signs of so many years under the sea and her bridge and upper deck structure has collapsed, making her somewhat difficult and unsafe to enter. Until the security regulations are changed, she will have to be left to the fish.

less reef damage and are easier for park personnel to maintain. Eventually, all of the sites will have these kind of anchors.

9 KARPATA

Location: *Northwest coast*
Depth: *23-120ft (29-32m)*
Access: *Boat*
Expertise Rating: *Intermediate*

Karpata is a true favorite of many knowledgeable Bonaire divers and snorkelers for its rich coral and sponge growth. It has a walk down 20 steps (seems like 50 going up!) to the beach and then there is part of a concrete pier that goes to reef's edge. The conventional wisdom of getting into the water, depending on wave height, is to make your way to the edge of the cement and then surf out over the rocky reef on an appropriate wave. Getting back is done pretty much the same way. One tip is to wade next to the slab where there is a slight channel and surf out from here. Snorkelers and divers may want to wear a dive skin at the very least to prevent getting scratched up.

A pair of four-eye butterflyfish

The park buoy here is moored with the old barrels in 23ft, which is where the reef already has some nice formations including stands of elkhorn coral. This is one of the few wall-like formations on Bonaire and it has steep rolling slopes and sand chutes with lots of coral cover. Turtle sightings and sleeping nurse sharks are common. The walls

Don't Touch the Coral

Wonder why you can't wear gloves and why touching the coral is such a big deal? The stony coral is the only animal in the world that can be injured or killed simply by being pressed against its own skeleton. Unlike the rounded bones of other animals, the skeleton of stony coral is razor sharp. The slightest contact slices living coral against its own skeleton.

The coral animals that create a coral head are only a few cell layers thick. To create a model of coral, think of a tissue draped over a razor blade, misted with water. Just as any contact would tear the tissue against the razor blade, so contact with stony corals slices the coral tissue against its own razor-sharp skeleton.

So Bonaire National Marine Park (BNMP) figures we should stay off the coral so our kids and grandchildren will be able to enjoy living reefs too!

also feature big sponges including tube and nice elephant ear sponges. There is black coral deep and flowing sea fans. Look for juvenile fish and cleaning action around the three anchors that are found on the reef.

A large variety of fish are seen here including the beautiful scrawled filefish, queen and rock beauty angels, endless processions of Creole wrasse getting cleaned and moving along the reef and, if you're lucky, schooling horse-eye jacks. Keep an eye out in the blue for eagle rays and other blue water critters. Up in the shallows, reef squid may be present. This site is really one of the Caribbean's finest. There is even a deep cave here past 120ft. Some dive shops come up here for a boat dive and make two dives here at the request of their guests. There are underwater tiles here that are part of a marine park experiment. Do not disturb this site or touch any part of it. The reef also has an old anchor embedded in the coral from days gone by.

Aside from the excellent diving, there are two constants about this site. People complain about the entry and exit. People also complain about theft from their vehicles. If shore diving, don't leave any valuables in your car or truck if you want to be as happy after the dive as you were during the dive.

A stoplight parrotfish sways with soft corals

10 | LA DANIA'S LEAP

Location: *Northwest coast*
Depth: *15-115ft (5-35m)*
Access: *Shore & boat*
Expertise Rating: *Intermediate & advanced, tech*

None other than the colorful Capt Don named La Dania's Leap. It seems one of his guests was a comely but rather aquaphobic lady named La Dania. She sought out Don's help to get her through her open water work with a demanding instructor. Don introduced her to his common sense, but unorthodox, methods.

'The sea,' he told her, 'is like part of us. As long as we can breathe and control our temperature, we can become part of this wonderful ocean.'

Her final dive of the week brought her to this cliff. Even though the instructor himself balked at the cliff entry, La Dania didn't hesitate.

'There was no delay,' says Don. 'Her mask came down. She made two steps to the ledge, cocked her knees, did a little spring, and forward rolled off that ledge into the incoming wave. That surprised me a little bit!'

Capt Don was so impressed he named that dive site for this group in November 1966. It became the famous 'La Dania's Leap' and is one of the most sought after reefs in Bonaire today.

Divers jump in here and drift to **Karpata** as the current normally runs that way.

Jump in the deeper water to the north of the park buoy and be prepared for a more difficult exit than entry. This is much easier as a boat dive, by the way, but not as much of a rush.

This also has the wall characteristics of **Karpata** and lots of marine life. There is a true drop-off here and wall. Way

Large star corals grow at Country Garden dive site

Juvenile spotted drums have flowing fins

down at about 135ft a deep reef can be used for tech training. Deep reef indentations that could loosely be called caves hold tarpon, big groupers and sleeping sharks in the 160ft region. But most people enjoy this site in the 60ft and above range for a fascinating drift ending at **Karpata**.

11	RAPPEL

Location: *Northwest coast*
Depth: *30-110ft (9-34m)*
Access: *Boat*
Expertise Rating: *Intermediate*

This site is a boat dive, as the name implies, and the cliff is not accessible unless you rappel. That's exactly what someone did and is how the site got its name. Bruce Bowker, one of the diving pioneers in Bonaire, and Stan Gdowksi, a mountaineer and diver who hailed from New Jersey, got together with dive and rappel equipment and trained to do the dive. According to Bowker's website, the two did this rappel in 1954 and the name has stuck ever since. He states it is easier getting into the water with full scuba gear than it is to rappel back up in full gear. And you thought **1000 Steps** was a tough dive!

The BNMP buoy here is in 36ft of water and most of the diving here is done in the 35ft to 70ft range.

Diving in the shallows can be tricky with an undercut from the 60ft high cliff appearing near sea level and continuing down 30ft more. It is an awesome sight, as waves crash into a white foam overhead. Then a sandy reef flat full of sea fans and flowing corals takes over. Look for flamingo tongue shells here.

Hard corals are abundant and schooling fish can be found in the protected areas. Coming up to the shallows, take care not to get too close to the cliff wall if there is strong surge. That is why at least intermediate training is good here. Or just make sure to follow your guide.

Most of the time it is a good place for exploration. Tubastrea corals grow along the rocks. This is a very popular dive site and guests request this boat dive virtually every week, so keep an eye on the boat schedule and dive from the mooring. It beats rappelling.

12 BLOODLET

Location: *Northwest coast*
Depth: *35-120ft (10-35m)*
Access: *Boat*
Expertise Rating: *Intermediate*

This is another boat dive with a deep mooring block and some moderate currents most of the time. This is good as the currents feed the abundant sponge growth along this slope. Good fish life is found here. Starting here and running down to **1000 Steps**, it is common to see the beautiful blue tangs in large schools eating algae and moving along the reef.

Different hard coral formations, including star coral, mingle with sponge formations. Yellow tubes in large clusters are found here. Look also for sleeping turtles and check the small cleaning stations for action.

As the mooring barrels are rather deep, move up to the shallows and look for nudibranchs and other invertebrates that have made their homes in the corals. Watch out for surge as well.

13 TOLO / OL' BLUE

Location: *Northwest coast, past the radio towers*
Depth: *10-130ft (3-35m)*
Access: *Boat*
Expertise Rating: *Novice*

If you come here you are already on the one-way road and must return home by driving north via the intersection down the road at **Karpata**. There is plenty of parking and a small lip raises the beach and sandy rubble. Just step down into the sandy area and make your way out. The buoy from the marine park is in shallow water at 16ft.

It is pretty evident why this is called Ol' Blue. This little bay has a sandy bottom leading to a gradual drop-off and the short swim out takes you past some staghorn coral and soft corals. From the boat, just head down to the reef.

The site has many fish, coral and sponges, including the ever-popular midnight parrotfish and the blue parrotfish. Plate corals intermingle with big boulders of star coral and there are

A blue tang has an azure spine

A grouper makes a meal of a bristleworm

many cleaning stations and eel holes. This is also a spot where lucky divers have spotted eagle rays.

The shallows here are good, with plenty of juvenile fish. Look for hermit crabs and other macro critters. Since the fish down deeper are a good size, the smaller juveniles are a nice contrast. One can off-gas here in the shallows for a long time. Snorkelers love this spot and often bring a picnic lunch and spend the day.

14	COUNTRY GARDEN

Location: *Northwest coast*
Depth: *15-120ft (4.5-35m)*
Access: *Boat*
Expertise Rating: *Novice*

This is a superb site, only reachable by boat, with some unique shallow water offerings and some great sponge life.

The mooring here is in fairly shallow water with the buoy at 19ft. The reef top is pretty with small star and brain corals and some small sea rods.

The reef falls off rather steeply and the current feeds a great variety of sponges. The reef bottom, where it goes into white sand, is rather deep at about 120ft or more. The sponge life here includes some large and very beautiful yellow and purple tube sponges, branching vase sponges, big stands of rope sponges and a few elephant ear sponges.

Layers of plate coral have encrusting sponges underneath in reds and purples. There are plenty of holes for spotted morays and even big green morays.

The shallow part of the reef near the 10ft to 20ft area may be the best part of the dive. Chunks of the cliff line have fallen in the water here and are adorned in sea rods and other soft corals. New growths of start corals are also found here. Shoals of goatfish and grunts hover, often schooling together, and a diver can swim past and through the many schools found around the boulders.

Close to the mooring there is also a beautiful large head of star coral that attracts chromis and other small fish. There are also purple sea fans present, and be on the lookout for marauding schools of blue tang that come through looking for algae patches to devour. They make a colorful photo subject if you anticipate their movements and get close for a photo.

15	BON BINI NA KAS

Location: *Northwest coast*
Depth: *10-100ft (3-32m)*
Access: *Boat*
Expertise Rating: *Novice*

Another boat dive along this rocky shoreline, the site name is actually a Papiamento (local language) greeting for 'welcome home.' If you dive this site a lot, you may feel like you are returning home. Just around the corner from

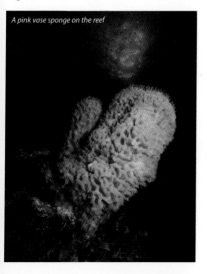
A pink vase sponge on the reef

the famous **1000 Steps**, this site is good for those who haven't done much boat diving.

The mooring is in shallow water at 18ft, and the reef slopes down, with the best diving in the intermediate range between 25ft to 60ft. This site also has some nice sponge life due to the very moderate currents that usually run here.

Look for turtles swimming by and for some larger parrotfish to cruise the reef. The endless schools of wrasse stop for cleaning action as they migrate down the reef.

16	1000 STEPS

Location: *Northwest coast*
Depth: *10-120ft (3-35m)*
Access: *Boat*
Expertise Rating: *Intermediate*

This is another of Bonaire's signature sites. Even if you don't dive or snorkel, go here to see the vista from the top of the steps. You can see the amazing blue water fade into the deep and look down the coastline to the mountains in the national park. If driving, park right by the entrance to the Radio Netherlands radio towers. If diving by boat, the buoy is in 21ft of water at the edge of the steep drop-off.

There are small shoals of fish in the shallows as you head out and then the reef drops off quickly. The fish life is also good along the reef with schools of male stoplight parrotfish coming here. Look for gray angels, tangs, doctorfish, schoolmasters and even ocean surgeonfish. There are lots of algae eaters here to observe.

The site is known for its clear water. Look for the black durgons in the water column. Many types of filefish, honeycomb cowfish, smooth trunkfish,

A banded or barber pole coral shrimp is found at a cleaning station

spotted rums and large white-spotted filefish can all be seen. Look also for sea turtles that seem to like the shallower water more so than the deep.

Exit back out through the sandy part of the inner reef and across the somewhat rubbly beach to the steps. Going down to the beach, there seems to be little debate about the number of steps. But the count on these steps on the way up is a different matter. The official number seems to be 68, although there are those that claim there are as many as 72 steps and as few as 64. But, if you have to haul your full dive gear back up after a long dive, it seems like 1000 by the time you're halfway up the flight.

This dive is a must for snorkelers and divers as well as beach bums wanting to enjoy the day. From this point on, the road is one way, so if you drive north, there is no turning back until **Karpata**. You can drive south from here on the narrow road back to **Oil Slick**, where the road gets wider and runs past the STINAPA Headquarters. There is also a very nice shoreline walk that runs from here to **Oil Slick**.

17 WEBER'S JOY / WITCHES HUT

Location: *Northwest coast*
Depth: *16-130ft (4-40m)*
Access: *Boat & shore*
Expertise Rating: *Novice*

This is a good site for photographers as it is an easy and non-sandy entry down a stone path that leads right to shore's edge. The beach is actually coral rubble, so enter slow and easy if beach diving. If entering from a boat, the shallow buoy is in 16ft. The upper reef has elkhorn and staghorn coral stands, so make sure you don't jump in on them. There are lots of chromis at reef top around the staghorn.

The reef drops quickly at 25ft and levels out in the sand at 125ft to 130ft. The nicest coral is in the 45ft to 80ft range just over the break of the slope, where there are large formations of mountainous star coral and great star coral. It is a good place to look for the purple-tipped sea anemones with their accompanying purple translucent cleaner shrimp and the delicate corkscrew anemones, also with shrimp. Octopus holes can be seen on the reef floor. Look for the broken shells and rubble by their doors.

This is a nice dive and also a very good spot for snorkeling. Look for colorful angels and parrotfish in the shallower waters. You may also encounter a few barracuda here.

18 JEFF DAVIS MEMORIAL

Location: *Northwest coast*
Depth: *10-120ft (3-35m)*
Access: *Beach*
Expertise Rating: *Novice*

This site from shore is a short walk down the coastal hiking path and then onto a rather small, rough beach. There's a ledge here, so to avoid a hernia, leave your gear on the ledge and hop down, then gear up. There's a sandy patch suitable for entry a little to the right, and the swim out is minimal. The mooring is shallow, in 15ft of water. This site also has some staghorns in the shallows, so watch where the boat swings so you don't jump in on them.

This place also has a nice collection of sea anemones with the colorful purple Peterson shrimp. The reef drops off quickly and has formations of corals and some sandy chutes that go down to the 120ft to 130ft range. The hard corals are interesting as they harbor squirrelfish, juvenile angels and barber pole shrimp in cleaning stations.

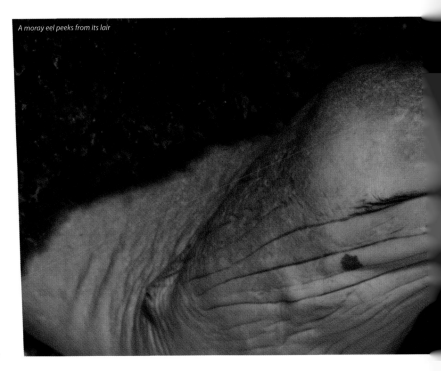

A moray eel peeks from its lair

The corals are mostly hard corals with a few fans and sea rods here and there. There are also nice sea plumes, porous sea rods and black sea rods. The best diving here is from 45ft to 75ft. The shallows have lots of chromis in the staghorns.

19 KALLIS REEF

Location: *Northwest coast*
Depth: *15-100ft (3-32m)*
Access: *Boat*
Expertise Rating: *Novice*

This is a newly opened site in the park that can be dived by shore or by boat. The buoy sits in 20ft of water. This site is named in honor of one of the marine park's champions, Kalli DeMeyer, a former park manager. She is still involved in many inter-island reef conservation projects.

There are beautiful soft coral formations on the rocky plateau below the small cliff shoreline. It is rarely dived and seems untouched.

The shallows look a lot like a pleasant combination of **Karpata** and the entry at **Oil Slick**. The swim out isn't far and the reef drops quickly around the 30ft mark.

The terrain is similar here to **Jeff Davis** with lots of hard corals and sand chutes. The sandy bottom appears at 130ft with more hard coral heads interspersed in the bottom terrain. There is lobed star coral, plate and sheet coral and lettuce coral around this reef along with rope sponges and some branching tube sponges. Well worth doing. This new park dive is destined to become a popular one.

A diver enters the water at Oil Slick Leap

20 OIL SLICK LEAP

Location: *Northwest coast next to park headquarters*
Depth: *20-80ft (5-24m)*
Access: *Shore & boat*
Expertise Rating: *Novice*

Unlike **La Dania's Leap**, this is only about a 4ft jump into the water, but seems higher. This site is right next to STINAPA Park headquarters and there is plenty of parking. The wooden pier and new ladder are courtesy of a sponsor, the Caribbean Club Bonaire. People come here to sunbake, snorkel and dive. The buoy is offshore in 28ft of water. The water at the entry is around 15ft deep. The ladder is the only way out so remember this and don't drift too far away from your exit point. You can also go in by ladder, but that's no fun … jump!

Snorkelers like this area as the shoreline wall has a series of small caves along the shallows. Since the area borders the stone shoreline, there is no sand beach, so visibility is always quite good.

The shallows have big gorgonians with a good collection of flamingo tongue cowries in the base of the branches. The reef starts sloping down at 20ft. Sea turtles like the hard coral

Seahorses

The seahorses found around Bonaire aren't always easy to see. They don't move much and take on the color of encrusting and small reef sponges, and are easily overlooked by the casual diver. Bring a small light and look for yellow, red, black or orange blotches on the reef, and then take a closer look. It never hurts to take a local guide if you want to find a seahorse. The guides usually know where they are congregating. This local knowledge saves you a lot of hunting time.

The seahorses are seen along the northern reef from **Small Wall** to **1000 Steps**, but can be found anywhere in these waters. They like the flowing stalks of the gorgonians. Seahorses are sensitive creatures and should not be harassed as they will move on and other divers won't be able to see them the next day. Please just look and don't touch. If you see a fat one, it may be a male carrying babies.

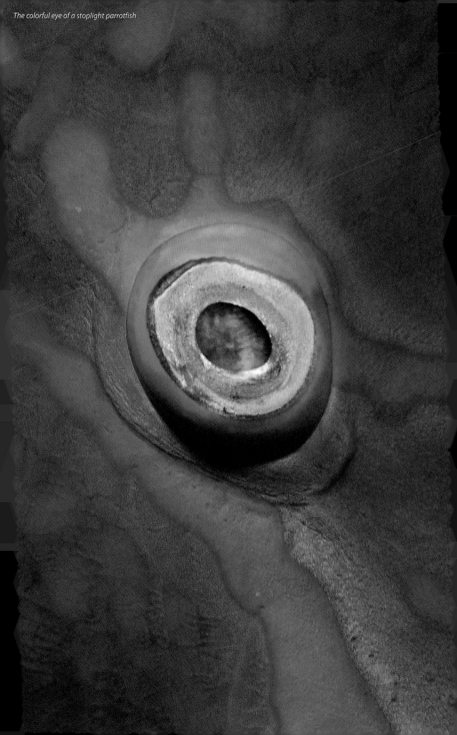
The colorful eye of a stoplight parrotfish

cover here and there is a nice fish population. Look for small barracudas staring
back at you. Also, remember to look in
the gorgonians for seahorses.

This is a very popular site and divers
and snorkelers alike repeat trips here
and enjoy it for night diving as well.
According to local historians, there
was never an oil spill or oil slick here.
It was once proposed as the site for the
BOPEC pier (now up next to Washington-Slagbaai Park) and the resulting
name stuck, even though the project
never happened.

staghorn coral. The gentle current here
means the gorgonians are feeding with
their polyps flowing in the surge: good
for video. Look also for lots of nice brain
coral formations.

Cleaning stations abound. Groups of
Creole wrasse come in to get cleaned
near stands of finger coral. Barber pole
shrimp sit in vase sponges and wait for
customers like graysbys and red hinds
to come in to clean. Fairy basslets hang
near large elephant ear sponges. This is
a nice, active reef with good hard corals. Look at the patterns on some of the
brain corals here – they are wild!

21 BARCADERA

Location: *Northwest coast*
Depth: *15-125ft (4-36m)*
Access: *Shore & boat*
Expertise Rating: *Novice*

This dive is a boat or shore dive and
since it is closer to town and the hotels,
you are getting into the area that dive
shops visit more frequently. This is also
a leap or ladder entry just north of the
hot flamingo-pink two-story house. The
mooring sits in 20ft of water and there's
lots going on at this reef.

The shallows have some nice sea
plumes and sea rods and a few stands of

22 ANDREA II

Location: *Housing area, northwest
coast*
Depth: *15-115ft (4-36m)*
Access: *Shore & boat*
Expertise Rating: *Novice*

There is some housing construction
going on here, so check with your dive
shop about any access changes to
this site. By boat, it is a simple matter.
The mooring sits in 15ft of water and
there is good snorkeling and a gradual
plain out to the drop, which is rather
deep. Yellowtail snappers and sergeant

A trumpetfish extends its snout to feed

A sand diver or lizardfish awaits prey

majors will probably greet you on your way down, as some fish feeding takes place here.

The soft corals are abundant, with tiny filefish hiding in the cover of the large sea plumes and sea rods. Flamingo tongues are also bountiful. Trumpetfish hide in the cover of the rods and the finger sponges, and seahorses have been seen here frequently. Spotted morays like the cracks and crevices.

Divers will find the drop-off starts deeper than most sites (at about 60ft) and goes down into competitive hard corals. Look for cleaning stations in the plate corals. Fish life is very good, including French angelfish, lizardfish, barracuda and lots of parrotfish. Even mantas have been seen here, so watch the blue.

This is a popular beach for snorkelers and divers alike of all experience levels. The ship *Aquaspace* also moors here on the middle buoy for snorkelers to enjoy the fish and marine life.

23	**ANDREA I**

Location: *Housing area, northwest coast*
Depth: *13-110ft (4-35m)*
Access: *Shore & boat*
Expertise Rating: *Novice*

This site is similar to the *Andrea II* site, with a sandy bottom and interspersed corals in the shallows. Occasionally

A dive boat moors at the drop-off

a turtle will swim through here, and also look for squid in the shallows. This whole reef area is just a bit sandier than its nearby cousin. This slope also goes down gradually and the sandy sea floor at 110ft has a group of garden eels. Watch for stingrays in the sand in the deep, and also look closely on this reef for small fluorescent flower corals.

This site is a favorite of fish watchers who report seeing doctorfish, blue tang schools, schoolmaster shoals, trumpetfish, triggerfish, midnight and stoplight parrotfish among many others. In the cracks and crevices a lobster or two has been seen at this site, as have seahorses.

Break-ins have been reported to vehicles from here so do not leave valuables in your dive ride.

Tube and other encrusting sponges grow at Town Pier

The House Reef Dive Sites

An iguana near the dive boats at Captain Don's

The House Reefs	GOOD SNORKELING	NOVICE	INTERMEDIATE	ADVANCED
24 PETRIES PILLAR	•	•		
25 SMALL WALL	•	•		
26 CLIFF	•		•	
27 LA MACHACA	•	•		
28 REEF SCIENTIFICO	•	•		
29 BUDDY'S REEF	•			•
30 BARI'S REEF	•	•		
31 FRONT PORCH	•		•	
32 SOMETHING SPECIAL	•	•		
33 TOWN PIER	•	•		
34 CALABAS REEF	•	•		
35 18TH PALM	•	•		

24	PETRIES PILLAR

Location: *Northwest coast*
Depth: *15-110ft (4-36m)*
Access: *Shore & boat*
Expertise Rating: *Novice*

Getting into the populated areas where many of the northern dive hotels and restaurants are situated, the reefs are often called house reefs. The diving on all of these is quite good with great fish diversity, nice selection of sponges and lots of cleaning stations. These reefs are fed from the deep channel between Bonaire and Klein Bonaire.

The marine park has designated from **La Machaca** down to **Calabas Reef** as shore dives only with the exception of **Something Special**, which has a mooring buoy. Some of these reefs are for hotel guests only, but a few allow visitors for a fee. Some want you to just check in and let them know you're diving and others ask you to sign a legal waiver of liability. Please check with the host hotel's dive center prior to making the dive to see what the current policy is on diving the desired house reef.

There are some very attractive pillar corals here, hence the name – given by the famous Capt Don – to a friend as a wedding gift. This is a lovely snorkeling site even though the park doesn't list it as so. This is not an easy entry or even easy to find, but it is easy going once in the water. The easiest way is to go by boat.

The shallows have stands of pillar corals and scatterings of other corals. Look for squid, queen and stoplight parrotfish, as well as nice staghorn coral. The drop-off begins near the area where the buoy anchor eye is drilled in 20ft and slopes down deep to 140ft. The slope is mostly hard corals and there are some tube sponges and rope sponges.

The upper reef is interesting and you may want to spend your time poking around the 20ft to 40ft area. Look for frogfish and glassy sweepers. Turtles seem to like this reef and you will probably see some greater soapfish as well.

25 | SMALL WALL

Location: *Black Durgon Inn, northwest coast*
Depth: *30-70ft (10-23m)*
Access: *Shore & boat*
Expertise Rating: *Novice*

The mooring sits in 24ft of water at Small Wall and the dive is best in the 30ft to 60ft range. As you face shore, the small, vertical wall that highlights the site is to the right. The shallows have many small fish complimented by stoplight, red-band and princess parrotfish. Look for bristle worms in the gorgonians. There are also juvenile spotted drums in the protection of the corals here.

An octopus changes color to blend in with its surroundings

The little wall is a beautifully land-scaped place with lots of sponge life, many small baitfish and trumpetfish roaming in and out of large growths of rope sponges. Macro critters like let-tuce slugs and spotted cleaner shrimp on giant and corkscrew sea anemo-nes make this a good place to narrow your focus. There are also spotted and golden morays in the various reef holes. Octopuses are also common here.

There are some nice invertebrates here like flamingo tongues, Christmas tree worms and brittle stars. Look for shoals of French grunts in the shallows.

26 | CLIFF

Location: *Hamlet Villas, northwest coast*
Depth: *30-70ft (10-23m)*
Access: *Boat & hotel pier*
Expertise Rating: *Intermediate*

This is the site of Capt Don's underwa-ter stone memorial that is dedicated to 'divers who have gone before us.' It is accessed from boat or shore with a shallow buoy in just 13ft of water. Snor-kelers can enjoy the shallows here with some elkhorn coral and lots of Spanish hogfish picking their way through the white sandy shallows.

There are some healthy purple tube sponges and also some orange ele-phant ears with fairy basslets hanging around them.

This little wall is great to dive early in the morning. As fish wake up, begin moving along the reef and start clean-ing at the cleaning station down the wall, the sun peaks over the wall tops and sends blue rays down through the clear Bonaire water.

Look for curious tarpon in this area. There are also lobsters found on this reef and a variety of moray eels.

A greater soapfish rests on the reef

27	LA MACHACA

Location: *Capt Don's Habitat, west-central coast*
Depth: *10-130ft (3-40m)*
Access: *Dock*
Expertise Rating: *Novice*

Entry here is from the small pier on the right of the Habitat property. Just swim out following a rope that runs to the drop-off and then all the way down the reef to 120ft. For those new to the area, just follow the rope out and back and it's hard to get lost. On the left of the rope is a small, upside-down fishing boat. Newer divers wanting to log a wreck dive can do so here. This is the *La Machaca* and it harbors all kinds of fish including mutton snapper and bluestriped grunts. At night, there are tubastrea corals that open their bright yellow polyps and make this little wreck a great spot to visit.

Critters that sometimes give divers a start are a large moray that sometimes lives in or around the wreck as well as some big tarpon that sneak up on divers at night.

On the reef below there are vase sponges with arrow crabs in residence. Look for the various corals like brain corals, finger corals and big stands of purple tube sponges.

Some sponges are growing right out of the brain corals on this reef. Way down deep on the south side of the

28 | REEF SCIENTIFICO

Location: *Capt Don's, west-central coast*
Depth: *12-35ft (4-11m) with a mini wall to 55ft (17m)*
Access: *Boat & shore*
Expertise Rating: *Novice*

The **Cliff**, **La Machaca**, Reef Scientifico and **Buddy's** are all close together and it is easy to purposely – or accidentally – swim from one to another. The science reference comes from an experiment where a grid was paid out at 40ft on this reef. Please don't disturb this site.

Look for similar terrain as **La Machaca**. Morays (green and spotted), parrotfish of all types, hogfish, angels and lots more are found here. Long processions of Creole wrasse seem to form a never-ending chain as they move up and down the reef in a long, strung out shoal. This is another favorite night-time dive.

29 | BUDDY'S REEF

Location: *Buddy Dive, west-central coast*
Depth: *10-95ft (3-30m)*
Access: *Boat*
Expertise Rating: *Advanced*

The reef at this popular dive resort is also good for all levels of divers and even some snorkeling action. This whole wall, starting at the **Cliff**, seems to get a constant but gentle current, keeping everything on the reef healthy.

The reef sits on a steep slope that starts at 30ft and runs down to sand at 100ft. Good sponge life, cleaning stations and lots of small and medium-sized hard

rope (affectionately called 'the highway' by Habitat staff) is another small shipwreck. The sand holds the promise of southern stingrays and garden eels, but it is quite deep.

Moving up top, there is a nice sandy area with lots of feeding hogfish and parrotfish.

There is also a small replica of one of the seven dwarves! Keep an eye out for a fully-grown great barracuda that seems curious about what you're doing at all times. Under the Habitat diver pier, there is always a school of tiny baitfish and an occasional octopus.

This reef is an excellent night dive and just one of the best in Bonaire. Have a beer at the Habitat bar after the dive and watch the sun go down over Klein Bonaire – the pizza is good too!

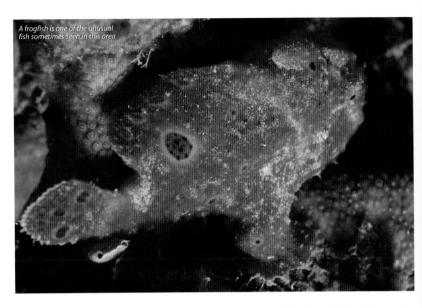
A frogfish is one of the unusual fish sometimes seen in this area

corals make this a great place to poke around. Some soft corals also punctuate the reef scene.

Look in the rope sponges and rocks for frogfish. As there are so many fish, this is very active at dusk and a late afternoon dive will deliver all kinds of sightings. Octopus, squid and turtles are also fournd at this site.

Dive classes are frequently done in the sandy upper reef area.

30	**BARI'S REEF**

Location: *Sand Dollar, west-central coast*
Depth: *3-110ft (1-36m)*
Access: *Shore*
Expertise Rating: *Novice*

A 'bari' is a barrel, and in this case it refers to a big barrel sponge found long ago in very deep water on this reef by a Bonaire explorer. Today Bari's Reef is used for all levels of diving and every depth is explored with fun discoveries to be had. Entry to Bari's Reef is made at the resort by beach, dock or ladder on the dock.

The sponges are still here, and more. According to the Reef Environmental Education Foundation (REEF) database, Bari has more documented fish species, a count of 317, than any other single reef in the whole of the Caribbean. Along with a few barrel sponges are tube sponges, elephant sponges, octopus sponges and vase sponges. The gentle current keeps the sponges healthy and brings in tarpon and barracuda to hunt for fish feeding in the nutrient rich environment. Even eagle rays coast by here.

Bring your macro lens. For small creatures, there's always the possibility of frogfish here. Even the rare goldspot eel may show up. Also, look for small wrasses around the reef floor, hogfish and peacock flounders. The rubble is also home to yellowhead jawfish. Look here for unusual blennies, like the redlip, and masked gobies. Take your fish checklist to this site.

This was once a junk dump and some of the stuff is still here. This provides great habitat for macro subjects. Poke around the junk, especially on night dives, and you may see some colorful and odd creatures.

| 31 | **FRONT PORCH** |

Location: *Sunset Beach, west-central coast*
Depth: *15-90ft (5-30m)*
Access: *Boat*
Expertise Rating: *Intermediate*

The former Sunset Beach site is the walk-in access here, at the time of this writing. The access is quite easy and by traveling either north or south, you will encounter different things on this reef.

The area has great fish diversity. Tarpon show up on night dives and barracuda are common by day. To the north there are coral heads and sponges with some open spaces in the reef.

Look at the rubbly bottom for goldspot gobies and yellowhead jawfish that incubate eggs in their maws. This makes for a great photo.

This area and south past **Salt Pier** has a sandy bottom and rubble that makes a conducive habitat for scorpionfish – so watch where you kneel or put your hands, especially at night. These fish use effective camouflage so take a second look at that rock you're about to touch.

On the south, there's an old anchor chain that leads to another old wreck, the New York tugboat. This old ship is also nice at night with some tubastrea growth on it that blossoms after dark with bright yellow polyps.

This ship is on the port side and the seabed around the wreck is good for macro life and small fish-like blennies and gobies.

Sea rods are among the reef's prettiest soft corals

Healthy growths of tube sponges are found in the BNMP

32 SOMETHING SPECIAL

Location: *South of Marina entrance, central coast*
Depth: *10-100ft (3-30m)*
Access: *Shore & boat*
Expertise Rating: *Novice*

This boat dive is also accessed by shore. The mooring is shallow, sitting in 10ft of water.

Divers like this site for the upper reef shallows as much as the deeper reef features. It is great for macro critters and the odd fish like frogfish. The fish diversity here is impressive.

On the right there is a sand chute that runs down the face of the reef slope and opens up into a broad sandy area full of garden eels. Look also for stingrays here. The reef going south is then covered in various corals along the wall. Most are low growing brain, star and plate corals. Some soft corals harbor small schools of French grunts. There are also scattered stands of branching vase and purple tube sponges. Keep an eye out for foraging spotted morays and juvenile spotted drums.

The upper reef is home to lots of open rubbly space and coral clusters. Look for hawksbill turtles poking around. The upper reef also has doctorfish surgeons, gray angels, yellowhead jawfish, sand tilefish and clown wrasses. This is a good spot for frogfish and they are usually in the 15ft to 30ft depths. Spotted scorpionfish, some very large, can be found in this habitat as well.

There seems to be a current flowing here all the time, making the area and its varied terrain a good place for a diverse fish population.

For the macro hunter, this is a superb spot. Keep an ear out for boats coming and going as they do come in quite shallow to moor.

33 TOWN PIER

Location: *Downtown Kralendijk, central coast*
Depth: *0-40ft (12m)*
Access: *Shore & boat*
Expertise Rating: *Novice*

Considered one of the must-do dives in Bonaire, this site is located right in the center of town. You can have a snack at City Café and then walk over and go diving. It is the smaller pier next to the big one in front of the old Dutch fort, and usually has a couple of ocean tugboats tied up to it. It can be done any time of day, but the colorful nature of the pillars that support the pier make most people go for it at night.

Since the large clusters of tubastrea coral and encrusting sponges grow right up to the surface, even snorkelers who are bothered by an overhead environment can enjoy this dive. The bottom looks like any pier area with smattering of junk. Some old tires have big stands of branching vase sponges in them. The undulating spotted rums and various assortment of moray eels like these trashy refuges, so look at each one as you will usually see some creatures of note inside or around the edges.

The dive is usually done under the safe confines of the pier itself. The sponge life is colorful, varied and healthy. You may see some filament lines around the pilings. Recently work was done and local volunteers took the sponges off the pilings and moved them to the reef until the work was completed. They then replanted them back to the pier. A lot of hard work went into the dive that tourists continue to enjoy.

The big draw is the heavy growth of tubastrea coral on the pillars. At dusk and at night the polyps open wide to feed, turning the pier into an Aztec

An arrowcrab rests on encrusting sponge at night at Town Pier

shrine of sun-yellow color and motion. On the sea floor and crawling on the pilings there are tons of arrow crabs. There are also different species of decorator and hermit crabs, bristle worms and octopuses.

This dive has special restrictions. It is only a shore dive and a certified guide must accompany divers and apply for your permission to dive here through the harbormaster. There have been limits placed on how many groups can dive here and the groups must be small, so apply early and often, to get your shot at this. Pick a guide who is good in marine creature behavior to get the best of this site.

34 | CALABAS REEF

Location: *Dive Bonaire and Carib Inn piers, west-central coast*
Depth: *15-125ft (5-22m)*
Access: *Boat*
Expertise Rating: *Novice*

This is the house reef for Dive Bonaire and the Divi Flamingo Resort. Carib Inn divers also use this as the house reef. Swim out past some anchors placed on the reef, presumably as fish attraction devices. The slope starts at

Save the Sponges

Tube sponges

In late 1988, renovations began on Bonaire's Old Pier, also called Town Pier or North Pier. In order to check for structural soundness, one out of every four of the 200 pilings beneath the pier was scraped bare of decades of growth, including sponges, orange cup corals, tunicates, tubeworms and even a few stony corals. The corals and tunicates weren't killed by being removed from their substrate, but they're not capable of reattaching.

But sponges, more primitive than corals and sea squirts, have no organs, and no systems. Sponges are basically groups of cells working together. 'Sponges,' I remembered Cathy Church telling me a few years earlier, 'can attach to anything if they're in firm contact with it long enough.'

That memory, and 50 denuded pilings, began the Sponge Reattachment Project. From May, 1989 until 1990, at least four sponges were tied onto a piling on every 'Touch the Sea' dive, in addition to the many dives dedicated solely to tying sponges. More than 600 sponges were tied onto pilings in the two years or so of the SRT Project. Almost all of them survived and flourished.

We had two advantages when working on the Sponge Reattachment Project in 1989. The pilings were completely bare, so we didn't have to worry about placing the sponges away from other growth, and the sponges were not removed from the pilings by any natural source.

The situation was quite different in 2004, after the storm surge from Hurricane Ivan rolled under the Town Pier. Ivan's waves didn't affect low-profile growth, such as stony corals and the like. However, sponge colonies that weren't firmly attached and sponge tubes with weak sections were knocked off by the waves.

The Sponge Reattachment Program, Phase Two, was led by Susan Porter (I was off-island at the time but sent suggestions). In several dives, Bonaire National Marine Park Volunteers tied dozens of sponges back onto pilings.

By Dee Scarr

about 30ft and runs down into the sand past 120ft.

This can be a wreck dive as there is a fishing type boat on the reef that attracts marine life. It sits at about 70ft deep off the Flamingo side of the reef. Look for small creatures like cleaner shrimp, nudibranchs and small morays in the clusters of coral heads. The site is usually home to bigger stuff, too, like tarpon and great barracuda. Look also for reef squid here.

Seahorses have been reported here in the past in the soft coral that is in the upper part of the reef. Look also for frogfish sitting in the rope sponges. Flamingo tongues are common in the sea plumes or sea rods.

35	18TH PALM

Location: *Plaza Hotel, west-central coast*
Depth: *15-120ft (15-30m)*
Access: *Shore & boat*
Expertise Rating: *Novice*

This is the house reef of the Plaza Hotel and can be dived by shore or by boat. This is also a nice snorkeling site. Entry is at one of the area's only sandy beaches and is just a walk in by a rock jetty that protects from most wave action. There is also a pier for Plaza guests at the Tipsy Seagull restaurant and bar. There is a school of smallmouth grunts under this pier all the time.

The mooring is offshore at 32ft. You will see that this is a unique reef as it flows down the slope into a sandy plain with a sand chute to the south. Across this plain is another deep reef at about 80ft that doglegs out and drops down some more. The dogleg runs into the slope at the south and a sloping reef runs south. This little outer reef leg usually has big fish with tarpon around in the blue and various mid-water fish schools moving about. Big jacks also come into view and eagle rays have been seen here.

Look in the reef and along the reef slope for lobsters, decorator crabs, batwing crabs, giant hermit crabs and lobsters.

The upper reef has been host to frogfish, though not consistently. The Toucan staff do intro and instruction here daily, plus a daily shore dive, so if you're staying here ask at the Toucan/Plaza dive shop about any new developments. It is also good place for macro critters like many colors of Christmas tree worms, flamingo tongues, arrow crabs and barber pole shrimp.

A curious great barracuda can stay with divers the whole dive

A seahorse at Something Special Reef

The Hilma Hooker shipwreck is the most famous of the southern dives

South Bonaire Dive Sites

Once you get to this point of the western coast of the island, the reefs are considered to be south dives. The shoreline and terrain here goes from flat to flatter, with the coastal road running down past the vast salt fields and the flamingo-breeding sanctuary.

This is not a very developed region. There are some homes and a few hotels down to the **Hilma Hooker** shipwreck area, and then it is pretty much open beach.

The coastal road gets narrower and becomes one lane as you drive further south. At some of the places it is very close to the actual shore break. These beaches are popular with kitesurfers, and history buffs also come here to see replicas of the old slave huts. There are many popular spots in this region and it is not unusual to drive down the road in the morning and see at least one dive truck parked in front of the coastal sites. This area ends at the southern tip of the island, where the wind and the wild seas make a scenic venue to watch the western sun sink into the sea.

If you're lucky, a 'V' of flamingoes will be winging south at dusk towards Venezuela.

South Bonaire Dive Sites	GOOD SNORKELING	NOVICE	INTERMEDIATE	ADVANCED
36 WINDSOCK	•	•		
37 CORP. MEISS / NORTH BELNEM	•	•		
38 BACHELOR'S BEACH	•	•		
39 CHEZ HINES			•	
40 LIGHTHOUSE POINT				•
41 PUNT VIERKANT			•	
42 THE LAKE	•	•		
43 HILMA HOOKER	•	•		
44 ANGEL CITY	•	•		
45 ALICE IN WONDERLAND	•		•	
46 AQUARIUS	•	•		
47 LARRY'S LAIR		•		
48 JEANNIE'S GLORY		•		
49 SALT PIER	•	•		
50 SALT CITY	•	•		
51 INVISIBLES	•	•		
52 TORI'S REEF	•	•		
53 PINK BEACH	•	•		
54 WHITE SLAVE	•		•	
55 MARGATE BAY	•		•	
56 RED BERYL	•	•		
57 ATLANTIS	•	•		
58 VISTA BLUE	•		•	
59 SWEET DREAMS			•	
60 RED SLAVE	•		•	

36   WINDSOCK

Location: *Flamingo Airport*
Depth: *12-100ft (3-32m)*
Access: *Shore & boat*
Expertise Rating: *Novice*

Since it's just past the airport, near the start of the runway, this site got its name from the telltale windsocks that are used to determine wind direction at airports. You can watch the planes land while you gear up at this coastal park, which is an easy walk-in at most of the park bench areas.

The site here is at the yellow painted rocks at the north end of the beach. Further down there's a small reef ledge that you must step down. The mooring for your dive boat sits in 29ft of water and is actually over the reef drop-off.

Divers have sighted blue spotted cornetfish in the shallows here; a sighting not all that common on other reefs.

The best snorkeling is reached by entering at the north end of the beach and heading towards Plaza Resort. For divers, head down the reef to the deeper

A stoplight parrotfish munches some coral

reaches and look for sea turtles and rays in the sand at 90ft. Work your way back up, checking the coral heads for blue-striped grunts, mutton snapper and yellowtail snapper as well as red hinds.

37	CORP. MEISS / NORTH BELNEM

Location: *Flamingo Airport*
Depth: *10-100ft (3-32m)*
Access: *Boat*
Expertise Rating: *Novice*

This is basically just the other end of **Windsock** where you can suit up at the park benches and step down over a ledge onto sandy and rubbly beach, then walk in over reef flats. The buoy here is in shallow water and the drop-off starts about 25ft and falls to 100ft.

The elkhorn coral is mostly skeletal but still holds protection and habitat for many small fish like damsels and juveniles. Going deeper, you will see some surgeonfish, different kinds of parrotfish and fairy basslets hiding in the cover of large, orange elephant ear sponges.

There are lots of morays in the various coral heads and French angels, barracuda and hamlets. Divers also report seeing basket stars unfolded and feeding atop the coral heads at night at this site. The sand is fine, so if the surf is coming this way, visibility can be lower and the exit a little cloudy.

38	BACHELOR'S BEACH

Location: *Past Flamingo Airport south*
Depth: *20-120ft (6-36m)*
Access: *Boat*
Expertise Rating: *Novice*

The entry from the beach can be quite tricky, as the stair set leading to the beach has a pretty long last step. But once you clamber down the steps or make your way to the left on the rocks down to the shore, the rest of the entry is easy and the swim is not far to the drop-off in about 25ft. The mooring buoy is in 13ft of water and an easier choice.

The upper reef has lots of flowing corals and small school of grunts and snapper. Peacock flounder also like the camouflage of this sandy bottom. The hard corals are also good and the reef is a mixture over the edge into the 30ft to 60ft range. Don't be surprised to see turtles here.

Tiger groupers, whitespotted filefish, smooth trunkfish, morays and queen angels are among the fish, so there is good diversity. The blue spot cornetfish has also been seen in these waters. This is another site that can be affected by the swell due to the fine sand here at the reef top. When the waves wash in, visibility decreases.

39	CHEZ HINES

Location: *Southwest coast*
Depth: *17-100ft (5-32m)*
Access: *Boat*
Expertise Rating: *Intermediate*

This is best done as a boat dive. At the time of writing, construction was being done at the beach entry with access difficult, but this may change. The mooring is fairly shallow at 17ft, and then the reef rolls down a gentle slope to the 100ft range where it is sandy again.

For the advanced divers, there is a deep reef area off in the sand at 110ft to 120ft, so watch your air going out. This again starts to drop off gently into the blue. This isn't a packed reef but has interspersed corals and coral head and some sandy patches. The ever-present garden eels can be found in the sand here, and also look for the possibility of a sleeping nurse shark, southern stingray, a white margate hunting in the sand, or – on the smaller end of the spectrum – sand tilefish.

This is a good area for all kinds of soft corals including the black sea rods and some sea plumes. Schoolmasters hang around these corals and French angelfish hunt around the area. While up shallow decompressing, look around for goldspot gobies.

This site is close to a point, so currents can be strong here, or they can pick up during a dive, so be aware of what is going on underwater.

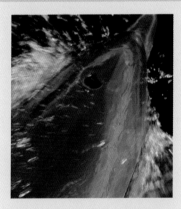

Bonaire's Dolphins

There are two types of dolphins commonly seen around Bonaire and Klein Bonaire; spinner dolphins *(Stinella longirostris)* and bottlenose *(Tursiops truncatus)*. They can normally be seen on boat dives going to and from the dive sites. Often they will try to ride the bow wave of a boat or play in large wake waves. Lucky divers have seen them around Klein Bonaire, where pairs of bottlenose sometimes come in to birth young. Dolphins are also seen at the south end of the island where currents converge and they follow fish schools and look for food. If you encounter a dolphin underwater, especially on scuba, it is a special event.

A trumpetfish can hover vertically

40   LIGHTHOUSE POINT

Location: *Lighthouse Beach Resort, southwest coast*
Depth: *16-115ft (5-32m)*
Access: *Boat*
Expertise Rating: *Intermediate to advanced*

There is shore entry at the tiny beach next to the Lighthouse Beach Resort. Please call in advance to see if there are any restrictions to entering here. This is also better done by boat, as the currents can be stronger on the point. Getting in and out can also be a chore, and it is wise to have a local guide show you the ropes at first.

This sandy slope drops down gradually, similar to **Chez Hines** with a bottom of sand at 115ft. Look for garden eels here as well. The currents feed the sponges and you can expect to find large barrel sponges and some candelabra vase sponges.

This is a good place for soft corals with nice sea plumes and others providing cover for young trumpetfish. Again, be aware of the currents, as they can change in strength during the course of the dive.

41   PUNT VIERKANT

Location: *Port Elizabeth*
Depth: *22-95ft (7-29m)*
Access: *Boat*
Expertise Rating: *Intermediate*

Bonaire's southern end has a famed double reef system. That is, there is the usual reef area growing along the shoreline drop-off that slopes down into deep sand, and another reef that runs south down the coast all the way to **Invisibles.** In some places this second reef, part of about 20 sites, is very close to the reef slope, and even joins it in some areas. At other points it is a very far and deep swim out from the slopes and runs deep, with some strong currents. Before heading out to look for a part of the deep double reef on any specific site, it is wise to dive the site with a local guide to get some bearings and knowledge. This site is at the start of the northern end of the double reef system.

For shore divers, the entry site is marked by the yellow park stones, but a construction project – moving very slowly at the time of writing – made access inconsistent. Sometimes the fence is open and sometimes closed, meaning this site is best done by boat. Currents here can also be tricky and stronger than most places on Bonaire.

The mooring sits in 22ft and the drop-off is nearby at 30ft. This site also has a gentle slope with soft corals and sponges. In the sand channel at 90ft are garden eels, and this is also a good place for stingrays, and perhaps some marauding pompano.

The double reef is deep at 90ft and seems to rise up if you are heading south. If you swim or drift this way for a while, you will find the reef actually curves in to meet the slope reef at 65ft to 70ft. This reef has lots of sponge life. Look for reef fish like yellowtail snapper, margate and bar jacks. The shallows have squid and peacock flounder.

A marine park ranger paints new dive site markers

Sponges and tube corals encrust the prop area of the Hilma Hooker

42 THE LAKE

Location: *Southwest Coast*
Depth: *13-130ft (20-40m)*
Access: *Shore & boat*
Expertise Rating: *Novice*

Most divers go here for a good double reef experience. Currents tend to be less than at **Punt,** and shore diving is simpler. The reef also comes in closer and is shallower, so divers can spend more time exploring. The shore entry is fairly easy through a sandy channel, although it is a long swim out. Divers used to have to enter here by driving their trucks

down from the **Hilma Hooker** entrance, but a new entrance from the main road marked by the yellow park rocks now makes this an easy site to get to with good parking at shore's edge.

The upper reef is full of soft corals, with stands of sea rods and some sea plumes. There are also some flowing gorgonian sea fans. Look for flamingo tongues here. But the best game plan is to head to the double reef first. This can be done by swimming directly in blue water, or by going down the slope to the sand in 80ft, swimming over the garden eels and up to the outer reef. It rises to 65ft and has lots of old growth hard coral. There are some big barrel sponges at the top of the reef, and large orange elephant ear sponges also grow here in

43 HILMA HOOKER

Location: *Southwest coast, north of TWR facility*
Depth: *20-100ft (6-32m), 62-100ft (19-32m) for 2 buoys on ship*
Access: *Boat*
Expertise Rating: *Novice (Deep: Intermediate)*

This site is so popular there are three buoys here. One on the reef at 20ft, one is on the bow at 80ft, and the other on the stern at 66ft. The parking area is large and you can see the trucks and some coral piles to gauge an exit. The only thing tricky is a reef flat lip right at the shoreline that can be a pain to step up and over with any kind of surf. Buddies may have to help one another a bit. To avoid the day boat crowds you may want to go here early in the morning or later in the afternoon. This is a popular night dive as well.

In its past, the *Hilma Hooker* was – among other things – a drug running ship, and at one stage 25,000lb of marijuana was found on board by authorities. It was purposely sunk and sacrificed to King Neptune for diving purposes in 1984. It is a 236ft (72m) long cargo freighter that has been pretty well stripped and has little to hang up divers. It lies on its starboard side, with the stern touching the reef and the bow slightly out into the deeper sand. The freight-hold faces out toward the double reef. Still, the wreck is deep and dark. A wreck penetration class should be taken before venturing inside. For the most part, the ship and holds are open and it is a pleasant dive to explore, with not much danger involved, if you keep an eye on your computer.

Doing this as a boat dive is much easier, as you're right there, and it's just a matter of descending the mooring line.

many spots. Look for sea turtles, plus blue water fish like silvery rainbow runners and even an occasional eagle ray.

The outer reef falls off into the blue well past 130ft. This reef has densely packed corals of all kinds. Look for sprawling brain corals, spiny flower corals and maze corals.

There are some coral patches that connect the two reefs. On the way back, look at the nice growth along the inner reef. There are some tube sponges and rope sponges. Bar jacks move up and down the reef. A few stands of staghorn coral provide good habitat for juveniles. Close to the mooring at 30ft there is a large coral head full of chromis that has a busy cleaning station. This is also a good night dive.

A young smooth trunkfish

The shore dive however, allows you to explore the inner reef on the way back, making your deco stop much more interesting.

Start at the deepest part of the ship and work into the shallower part. The bow is in about 100ft in the sand. Look underneath the bow for colorful tubastrea corals. At night these are as pretty as the ones at **Town Pier**. The hull is fairly clean but the forward bridge area has abundant sponge growth. Yellow encrusting octopus sponge and big, purple tube sponges grow all around the bridge.

There are usually a few big tarpon cruising and hovering around the wreck. On the reef side, lots of chromis and other small fish swim in the water column by the bow. A mast sits out in the sand.

The center holds are open and adorned in sponges. The aft area has some davits and railings with small coral growth. But the best part of the aft is the prop and the big rudder. On top, sponge clusters grow on the prop shaft and blades. Underneath, big purple tube sponges, red and yellow encrusting sponges and tubastrea corals adorn the hull and are worth seeing, day or night.

From this area, at about 70ft, head up the reef if you are shore diving and enjoy the upper reef. Plate corals and schools of smallmouth grunts are in the 30ft to 40ft area. Soft corals with schoolmasters and hiding stoplight parrotfish can be seen up top.

Some divers also go over to the double reef after seeing the shipwreck. This is easier done for boat divers. The double reef is in the 70ft to 80ft area.

44 ANGEL CITY

Location: *Next to Hilma Hooker, southwest coast*
Depth: *28-80ft (8-24m)*
Access: *Shore & boat*
Expertise Rating: *Novice*

Yes, there are angelfish at Angel City, but there's a lot more as well. An easy beach entry and a mooring that drops you right over the drop-off make this a snap to get to. This and adjoining **Alice in Wonderland** may be one of the best places on Bonaire to get a good look at the double reef in moderately shallow water. If shore diving, there is usually a big coral stone beach marker, and it is a long swim out, but you start seeing coral about halfway out to the drop-off, so there is something to check out as you come and go.

Head down the reef where the sand appears at only 60ft. This sand area is quite interesting, with queen conchs, southern stingrays and lots of small coral gardens waiting to be found. The double reef is just a short swim across and rises to 60ft to 65ft, with lots of hard corals and nooks and crannies that hold

A BNMP yellow rock marker shows the way to each beach dive site

all kinds of marine life. Look for the roaming tarpon, porgies and eels in the many holes. Mating porcupine puffers have also been seen playing their odd game here. At many places, the double reef merges with the slope reef.

The coral growth is very competitive here. You will see finger coral growing into large brain corals. The upper reef has appealing soft coral. It is a long swim back but there's lots of coral to see during about half of that swim. There are many small hard corals through here, and the fish and corals are as diverse as any place on Bonaire. This is a great place to hunt for juveniles, gobies and blennies. Nudibranchs are in here too. Divers have been known to repeat this dive more than once during a trip.

45 ALICE IN WONDERLAND

Location: *North of Salt Pier, southwest coast*
Depth: *16-100ft (4.5-30m)*
Access: *Shore & boat*
Expertise Rating: *Intermediate*

Although the site is close to **Angel City**, this is a decidedly deeper dive and also much different. Entry from the shore is easy and the park buoy is up on the reef flat before the drop-off. There is a lot of coral at the drop-off, both hard and soft, and a multitude of cleaning stations and small fish schools. It is a good place to snorkel with a sand path right to the entry.

The slope goes down to sand at about 80ft and there's a long crossing to the outer reef, which tends to run deeper as you go south. So watch your computer if this is the way you go. The outer reef has the thick coral growth and lots of cover, and sometimes sea turtles come into the area. There can be a current. Most local dive masters swim in a square here, moving across sand, then going along the outer reef, then crossing again about halfway through the dive and coming back along the reef slope with the current at a shallower depth.

If you're just into poking around, there are some nice coral clusters in the middle of this sand channel. They look like sculpted gardens in the white sand. Big green morays and graysbys can be found.

Up on the slope, you may see more eels. The sponge life is good, with barrel sponges, tube sponges and elephant ears all present.

Higher up, schoolmasters live around the hard corals. Lobed star coral, finger coral, plate coral and sheet coral can all be found as well. There are some big coral rock mounds on the beach to help you find your way back in.

46   AQUARIUS

Location: *North of Salt Pier, southwest coast*
Depth: *15-100ft (6-16m)*
Access: *Shore*
Expertise Rating: *Novice (first reef), advanced (second reef)*

This is a shore-only dive and an easy entry with a nice, sandy beach. There is a long, sandy reef flat and it is a rather long swim out. The slope starts to go down at 25ft and hits the sand at 100ft. For most divers, this slope is where you will spend most of the dive. Look in the sand for hovering cornetfish.

The slope is full of various hard corals and there is an interesting variety of smaller fish, angels and grunts. Sponge life is also healthy. Look for lavender tube and orange elephant ear sponges. There are some large brain corals here and sheet corals.

For divers trained in compass navigation, or those with an experienced guide, the second reef is one that must be navigated. It is far out and deep, with the top in the 90ft to 100ft range. Big jacks, eagle rays and sea turtles can be seen here. This reef also has good hard coral density and sponge life. Take note of the current, as you are really out far and deep. If you're not absolutely sure what you're doing, stay at the inner reef as there is plenty there to keep you occupied.

47   LARRY'S LAIR

Location: *North of Salt Pier, southwest coast*
Depth: *15-100ft (4.5-30m)*
Access: *Shore*
Expertise Rating: *Novice*

You're getting close to the **Salt Pier** now, and the reef flat is broader and sandier. There isn't a big parking area and the beach can be rather rocky except for one sandy spot that leads onto the reef flat. The swim out also has some corals to go around.

This dive is similar to the one next door, with the double reef being pretty far out and deep, and also hard to find at times because the sand is fine and visibility can be lower than at some other spots. But on Bonaire, that's still very good. Dive the second reef at this site with an experienced guide and make sure you have a lot of experience as well. The reef starts down at 30ft to 35ft and bottoms out at 100ft. The sponges are again prevalent and diverse. Frogfish have been reported around some of the sponges, and eagle rays have been seen too. Look for schools of grunts and goatfish, sometimes together, swimming along the reef or hovering near a coral cluster.

Pink flamingoes have a southern sanctuary
that airplanes are not allowed to fly over

48 JEANNIE'S GLORY

Location: *Close to Salt Pier, southwest coast*
Depth: *30-100ft (9-32m)*
Access: *Boat & shore*
Expertise Rating: *Novice (first reef only)*

This dive is similar to **Larry's Lair** except the double reef starts even deeper at the 130ft mark, which is the sport diving safe limit. So we suggest the dive be made on the reef slope. This site is also a boat dive, with the mooring at 20ft over the reef flat leading to the drop-off.

Getting in isn't so bad, but there's a shelf past the entry so inflate your BC or you'll find yourself up to your chest quickly. It is a long swim out to the drop-off at 35ft, and this is also a place where the sand is fine. Look for peacock flounder in the shallows and a few wrasse and hogfish. You'll first see a lot of soft coral growth that is good cover for juvenile fish and perhaps a juvenile filefish.

The sand is at 105ft to 110ft. There is attractive sponge growth, soft corals and various hard coral clusters with cleaning stations and chromis up in the water column. This reef also has collections of the purple-tipped giant anemone and some corkscrew anemones. Check each for glass, bobtail and Pederson shrimp.

49 SALT PIER

Location: *Under the Salt Pier, southwest coast*
Depth: *14-60ft (4-18m)*
Access: *Shore*
Expertise Rating: *Novice*

The same rules apply here as they do at **Town Pier**. You must have a certified dive master apply for permission to lead you here. So if you want to go, con-

Flowing sea fans at reef top

Diving between the pillars at Salt Pier

barracuda hover and follow divers. Goatfish school under the pilings, as do French grunts and schoolmasters. Soapfish laze on the coral and trumpet-fish try to blend in with rope sponges. There are also eels and octopuses to be seen. The bottom has some junk that is a great habitat for crabs and juvenile fish. People love this dive day and night and it is shallow, so a nice, long dive can be made. Try one dive with wide-angle and another with macro to bring back memories of the best of both worlds.

50	SALT CITY

Location: *Directly south of Salt Pier*
Depth: *21-60ft*
Access: *Shore & boat*
Expertise Rating: *Novice*

This is one of those long swims out if you're not making a boat dive, and the entry is pretty rocky. If you're boat diving, the mooring is near the drop-off at 21ft. Just head down the slope from the mooring and you'll see the double reef. Like the dive at **Angel City**, this is a good place to explore the various facets of the double reef system and get a look out into blue water at the second open ocean drop-off for big jacks, rainbow runner or a sea turtle.

The reef top for the second reef is only about 60ft and actually gets shallower as you swim to the south. Going north, it starts to get deeper.

This shoreline reef slope is again pocked with corals, sponges and soft corals, with a good amount of fish life hanging around. Even right at the drop-off, it is a pretty interesting section of reef to explore. This can be a rewarding, long exploration. Don't forget to check out the garden eels in the sand at 75ft. Divers also report seeing one or more eagle rays here on occasion.

tact your favorite guide and give him a few days to get it done. The going rate for both dives is between $25 to $30, depending on who you talk to. The usual entry/exit is on the north and is smooth going. There is a broad sand plain that slopes gradually. It's okay to start the dive early, as you may see small sand critters in this area. Also, be aware that scorpionfish like this habitat, so watch where you step. Good buoyancy is the key.

This maze of pillars can be confusing, especially at night, so just enjoy the dive and let the guide do the work. This is a good mid to late afternoon dive with the sun starting to head lower in the west. Anytime after 2pm gives wide-angle photographers the opportunity to get the sun's rays filtering through the support pillars. Some nice close focus wide-angle work can be done with candelabra, rope and tube sponges growing from the supports. This is really a fun place to compose and try various exposures.

The sea floor also has a nice assortment of fish and invertebrate life. Great

51   INVISIBLES

Location: *South of Salt Pier, southwest coast*
Depth: *19-130ft+ (6-40m+)*
Access: *Shore & boat*
Expertise Rating: *Novice*

Hey snorkelers! Garden eels in only 20ft of water! This site is good for all levels of divers and is one of the island's most diverse. If the swell is down, snorkeling can be very clear. Swell stirs up the sand a bit and makes entry and snorkeling a bit harder.

Sitting at the south end of the double reef system, you can visit both reefs here, plus some pretty coral oases in the middle of the sandy channel between the two reefs. There is a sand chute that you can follow down to about 80ft and proceed from there to the coral islands or the double reef. The double reef top is at about 80ft and slopes quickly to 130ft, and more on the outside of the reef, so this can quickly become a deeper dive than planned on. Watch your computer.

The reef slope and hard and soft corals hold everything from seahorses to

A coney sits in the reef

frogfish and many of the usual suspects as well. Look for various groupers and horse-eye jacks cruising for a meal and occasionally going after some smaller fish. This whole reef going up the slope has lots of surprises, so this site may warrant a deep dive and also another shallow dive to see everything the site has to offer.

52   TORI'S REEF

Location: *Right of Intake Channel, southwest coast*
Depth: *22-95ft (6-30m)*
Access: *Shore & boat*
Expertise Rating: *Novice*

Be prepared for a long swim out. People shore diving enter two ways here. Some go over the reef flat next to the channel that is an intake for the salt fields. Others just go into the intake channel (when it's not intaking) and swim out. There is a long swim out that divers may enjoy and snorkelers can spend a lot of time at as well. Look for reef squid in the shallower water.

Past the buoy the reef slopes at 30ft to 35ft and bottoms out at 95ft. The reef slope is gradual.

There are nice sea anemones here and other invertebrate life. Look for some lobsters and also barber pole shrimp at the cleaning stations. Goldentail morays and spotted morays like the cracks and cover here as well.

This is a fishy reef with saucereye porgies, fish like schoolmasters and smallmouth. Rock beauties, French angels and queen angels have all been seen here.

The Creole wrasse schools move up and down the reef and stop at the cleaning stations. Look also for juveniles like spotted rums. There are also a few scorpionfish on this reef.

Historic white slave huts sit right on the beach

53   PINK BEACH

Location: *Beach Park with palms, southwest coast*
Depth: *15-100ft (4.5-30m)*
Access: *Shore & boat*
Expertise Rating: *Novice*

The Cargil Salt Company donated this stretch of beach, and it is a fantastic place to watch the sunset and pelicans while enjoying a sundowner. The coconut trees are permanently bent facing west due to the wind. There aren't a lot of palms on Bonaire (mostly cactus), so this site has a tropical feel. The entry marker is at the north end of the beach, and the entry is fairly easy. The exit could be complicated by the reef lip at the beach, as it's a little tough to negotiate if there is any surf.

The park mooring is in 15ft of water and the reef flat is a long swim to the drop-off at 30ft. It runs down to 100ft and a sandy plain. It goes from soft corals and sea fans to hard corals down deep.

Look for the elusive sand tilefish out in the sand and – you guessed it again – garden eels! Southern stingrays are also found in the sandy channel.

Like **Tori's**, this is a good place for fish, with jolthead porgies, trumpetfish, schooling blue tangs looking for algae patches, the occasional cornetfish and seemingly a lot of porcupine puffers.

It is a good afternoon dive or snorkel before enjoying the sunset and possibility of flamingoes flying in.

Schoolmasters hover at the Hole's reef top

water. Dive this site on a sunny day; it is stunning. You will notice a few tarpon, then more, and then you realize there may be 50 or 100 tarpon just hanging and glistening in the sun. It is an amazing sight. The sea floor is littered in sea fan skeletons. They are decomposing into sand and providing habitat for small fish. The sea floor is also home to rays and queen conch, one of the few places you may still see one in the wild around Bonaire.

There are overhangs and small caves with cleaning stations. Tiger groupers, puffers and trumpetfish all hide in these recesses. Look also for French and queen angelfish and various parrotfish and rock beauty angels. Goatfish, snapper and chubs all hang together. Sea rods decorate the reef wall all around the hole. Further down the wall a big shoal of schoolmasters is accompanied by a few photogenic porcupinefish. And even further down the reef, hundreds of horse-eye jacks form a cloud over the hole.

This is a great wide-angle dive and it has superb macro as well. One of the Caribbean's finest dives, it is exited by going over a field of sea fans and out to mooring number 62.

Larry's custom boat heads for the Cai Channel

64	CAI

Location: *Cai Channel, southeast*
Depth: *25-120ft (7-36m)*
Access: *Boat (BNMP site 63)*
Expertise Rating: *Intermediate to advanced*

Again, the safest and sanest way to do this dive is by boat. This is because this is the main entry and exit for water coming into Lac Bay. Aside from incoming and outgoing tides, which aren't normally too dramatic, there is also the

Snorkeling inside The Lac blue waters is very good

Bog lobsters may also be hiding here. The record for eagle rays sighted by a wildside dive master is 51 in one big squadron. Ocean triggerfish sometimes nest in this area as well.

As you drift past the channel mouth, the terrain has more ridges and sand valleys and the corals seem to be in larger groups with finger, star, lettuce and brain corals all in clusters. This provides good hiding places for French angels, French grunts and squirrelfish. Look for many black durgons and other fish in the water column. End the dive by drifting out into the blue to avoid the inshore surge and have the boat pick you up.

65 BOKA WASHIKEMBA

Location: *Washikemba coast, south-east coast*
Depth: *25-140ft (7-44m)*
Access: *Boat (no buoy, not an official park site)*
Expertise Rating: *Intermediate to advanced*

This is a bit of a boat ride up the wildside coast to an area that has a lagoon and interesting shoreline with a reef flat that travels far out before falling into deep water. This part of the island is rarely dived and there is a good chance of seeing reef blacktip sharks and nurse sharks on every dive.

Drifting here is also quite pleasant, with seemingly endless fields of beautiful purple sea fans. The diver can explore this undersea forest and see other smaller corals and fish hiding in the fan fields. There are spotty mounds of big hard corals and the blue again has barracuda and the chance to see squadrons of eagle rays and even a manta ray.

Since this is a drift, exit in blue water and the boat will pick you up.

water pushed over the reef by wind-driven waves and natural surf. This water is looking for a way out and the channel is where it exits. This causes a rip current that can flow north and south as well. Only experienced guides know how to handle this, so it is by far safer and easier to go by boat, even when it is calm. If you do try this from the beach, make sure someone knows when and where, so if you get swept away, they'll know to come look for you after a few hours.

The entry to the bay channel is through a fairly shallow cut in the reef at the conch shell hills by a small, wooden pier. The boat normally goes a bit south to get into good visibility, as the actual channel can have poor visibility (another reason to boat dive).

But the dive itself gets better as the drift goes on. The reef in front of the bay mouth itself and running south has some big sea fans and sea rods (more in the shallows than deep), elkhorn corals, coral islands and a marine slope to 120ft. The dive is normally in the 35ft to 70ft range. Look for tarpon (sometimes in pairs or groups), sea turtles, eagle rays and nurse sharks nestled into the coral heads or down in the deep sand.

66 | BOKA SPELONK

Location: *Washikemba coast, south-east coast*
Depth: *25-140ft (7-44m)*
Access: *Boat (no buoy, not an official park site)*
Expertise Rating: *Intermediate to advanced*

Spelonk is one of the few wall sites along the coast and it has plenty of action. A boat dive only, this is a pretty special trip and worth the extra travel time, as all kinds of blue water fish come in here. It is the easternmost tip of the island and it attracts many species.

This is a wonderfully fishy site, with wahoo, rainbow runners, yellowfin tuna and mahimahi all seen on dives here. The drift is normally done at about 70ft along the cliff line wall. The bottom is weedy but also has hard corals. This is one of the few places on Bonaire where queen and ocean triggerfish are common. Also, Nassau groupers are found here and are normally very big. Blacktip sharks are one of the attractions of Boka Spelonk and are usually seen on every dive.

There are some pieces of wrecks at 70ft to 80ft. These wrecks, located at the base of the now-defunct old Spelonk lighthouse, are considered the island's best shipwreck array. They lie near the cliffs that created their demise, with huge boulders and a sandy floor making a brightly lit maze among the ships. There are tunnels and caves in the sheer of the cliff. Some dive shops will venture up here in the calm months. This is the best dive on Bonaire to see open-ocean fish. Mantas, hammerheads and even tiger sharks are a possibility at this unique dive site.

The Wildside folks consider this one of the better exploratory dives. They are

Snapper school above healthy coral

also considering some exploratory diving at the north tip during calm season. The area of Malmok, the northernmost point on Bonaire, is nothing but blue water. Then there's ocean, uninterrupted for a thousand miles into the northern Caribbean. The possibility of diving with bull sharks and hammerheads, something that is becoming popular in the Bahamas and other Caribbean sites, is one of the goals of exploration in the far north.

A diver watches a silvery tarpon

SNORKELING LAC CAI

There are a couple of good places to snorkel that will show you the magical world of the inner lagoon and mangrove swamp as a natural ocean incubator. On the southern side of Lac Bay is Sorobon, popular with windsurfers. There is easy shore entry from the sandy beaches; just keep an eye out for the windsurfers. There is a reef out toward the mouth that is designated for snorkelers and kayakers, and there are kayak moorings here. In this area by the surf line you will see a collection of hard corals with healthy and populous brain corals. The bay and reef have small and large turtles (though not as frequently seen as the outside). There are surgeonfish, angels, groupers, schoolmasters and many species of juvenile fish, as well as finger-sized barracuda. Some people like to night snorkel here as well.

The mangroves hold an unusual and eerie world, with barnacle-covered roots, upside-down jellyfish *(Cassiopea xamachana)*, tiny anemones and an occasional queen conch all part of the sandy and plant-covered bottom. Wear a skin to protect you from the sun and the marine creatures. The jellies and anemones can sting. You must have a trained biologist or naturalist from one of the kayak tours or nature excursions show you this weird mangrove world. Watch your fins in this environment. The breeding areas are fragile and should not be disturbed or kicked, so move slowly and carefully. This whole Lac is very shallow.

A bottlenose dolphin swims over the reef at Monte's Divi

Klein Bonaire Dive Sites

Klein Bonaire is the flat, little uninhabited island off the central west coast of Bonaire that is a paradise for snorkelers and divers, and also a popular destination for day-trippers.

Every day, boats carrying beachgoers and divers head out to visit the 26 marine park sites on the island. Many just head to **No Name Beach** to laze in the white sand and soak up the rays. Others enjoy the deep dives in the channel between the islands, or the beautiful corals off the western end of Klein.

Snorkelers use the moorings here and go to some of the very rewarding sites in the protected bay areas, where coral is thick and the water clear.

This island is now a reserve and a sea turtle hatchery. Sea turtles use the beaches of the island to make nests and lay eggs. Thus, only a small portion of the island and its beaches are open for public use, and the rest is set aside for turtles and to let the natural flora and fauna grow.

This island has a rich history in the diving world and was once privately owned. In 1939, German dive pioneer Hans Has explored and photographed it. In 1966, American John Bogart bought the island for $15,000. He and Bonaire's scuba pioneer, Capt Don Stewart, intended to develop Klein Bonaire. The island was overrun with goats, so Capt Don organized the 'Great Goat Round Up.' The past 33 years have now been goat-free and the natural flora has been able to make a comeback.

More recently, other development plans surfaced, and in 1996 a group of concerned citizens – led by longtime Bonaire naturalist Dee Scarr – met to save the island.

Money was raised from various sources (mostly private and through help from the Dutch government) to buy the island and give it back to nature, to ensure healthy reefs, turtle and waterfowl nesting grounds would be open and native plants and animals could thrive.

The government of Bonaire has plans for the island to become one of the Antilles National Parks, whereby it will remain untouched forever. However, the remainder of the money necessary to pay for it and formalize park management must now be raised.

Divers mostly dive here in the mornings but afternoon and night dives here are excellent.

Klein Bonaire Dive Sites	GOOD SNORKELING	NOVICE	INTERMEDIATE	ADVANCED
A NO NAME BEACH	•	•		
B EBO'S REEF				•
C JERRY'S REEF			•	
D JUST A NICE DIVE			•	
E NEAREST POINT			•	
F KEEPSAKE			•	
G BONAVENTURE	•	•		
H MONTE'S DIVI	•	•		
I ROCK PILE	•	•		
J JOANNE'S SUNCHI	•	•		
K CAPT DON'S REEF			•	
L SOUTH BAY	•	•		
M HANDS OFF	•	•		
N FOREST	•	•		
O SOUTHWEST CORNER	•	•		
P MUNK'S HAVEN	•	•		
Q TWIXT			•	
R SHARON'S SERENITY			•	
S VALLERIE'S HILL	•	•		
T MI DUSHI	•	•		
U C H ANNEX / YELLOWMAN			•	
V CARL'S HILL			•	
W EBO'S SPECIAL			•	
X LEONORA'S REEF	•	•		
Y KNIFE			•	
Z SAMPLER	•	•		

A blue parrotfish, accompanied by a jack, swims over the reef

A | NO NAME BEACH

Location: *Klein Bonaire*
Depth: *6-80ft (2-25m)*
Access: *Boat*
Range: *Novice*

It is the one site on Klein Bonaire where there is actually a beach dive. There are a bunch of moorings in the shallows in depths of 6ft to 16ft, with most in 10ft of water. The Samur mooring is off in 180ft,

and is for a private sailboat that goes there for day and sunset dinner cruises.

Divers and snorkelers can explore the corals and many hand-fed fish that live in the sandy shallows. Some come right up hoping to be fed some sort of handout.

Due to the sand, it is not heavily overgrown with coral, even on the slopes. So most divers prefer other Klein sites with denser growth. It is a good intro-dive, or good for someone taking classes. There is a sandy bottom, so flounder, some rays and other sand-dwellers, like goatfish, can be seen.

B EBO'S REEF

Location: *Klein Bonaire*
Depth: *20-120ft (6-37m)*
Access: *Boat*
Range: *Intermediate or novice with guide*

C JERRY'S REEF

Location: *Klein Bonaire*
Depth: *15-130ft (4.5-40m)*
Access: *Boat*
Range: *Novice*

Around the corner to the south from the mellow **No Name** is Ebo's Reef, a favorite of divers and a very photogenic reef for underwater photo buffs. Don't meet your buddy at the bottom of the mooring, as it sits off the channel in 140ft of water. The slope here is steep and full of loose sand and coral, with scattered corals and also some areas of heavy growth.

Expect a lot of fish life here. The scattered reef provides habitat for a great number of fish. Many of these are juveniles like tiny boxfish and reclusive ones like spiny puffers.

As the reef faces the open channel between Klein and the main island, there are lots of fusiliers, clouds of chromis, jacks and parrotfish. This reef and the next one over, **Jerry's**, are known for their sponge life. Big elephant ears and tube sponges can be found here. Look also in the deeper parts for black coral. There is usually a current running over this reef and crinoids feed in the current, as do the soft corals.

This reef also has the base of the mooring buoy down deep in 130ft of water and has similar terrain to **Ebo's,** with some beautiful black coral trees and amazing stands of rope sponges, purple tube sponges and the orange elephant ear sponges.

The site was named after a local photographer, Jerry Schnabel, who used to prefer this reef to do wide-angle photos with the nice sponges here. So wide-angle shooters, take note; if it is good enough for the pros, it must be a good spot. It is also excellent for fish photos and macro.

This site also has many juveniles and a lot of cleaning stations with the beautiful scarlet lady shrimps. There are purple-tipped anemones with Pederson shrimp on board, and this site also has black feather crinoids.

Look for masked gobies on the sponges. Flamingo tongues can be found clinging to sea plumes in the shallows and blacktip sharks have been seen, albeit rarely, in the shallows here as well.

A colorful barred hamlet

D JUST A NICE DIVE

Location: *Klein Bonaire*
Depth: *20-130ft (6-40m)*
Access: *Boat*
Range: *Novice*

This site is currently closed to diving and snorkeling.

E	**NEAREST POINT**

Location: *Klein Bonaire*
Depth: *20-130ft (6-40m)*
Access: *Boat*
Range: *Novice*

F	**KEEPSAKE**

Location: *Klein Bonaire*
Depth: *20-130ft (6-40m)*
Access: *Boat*
Range: *Novice*

This site is currently closed to diving and snorkeling.

G	**BONAVENTURE**

Location: *Klein Bonaire*
Depth: *20-130ft (6-40m)*
Access: *Boat*
Range: *Novice*

Before the northern dive hotels were built, this was the closest Klein dive site from Bonaire, hence the name, which has stuck for years. The mooring here also falls into deep water, but the boat usually swings in over the reef due to the wind.

The top of the reef is attractive, with lots of hard corals and schools of goatfish, snapper and chromis. Dropping down over the edge at about 30ft, the reef is famous for large elephant ear sponges. But there are also impressive stands of purple and bright yellow tube sponges, some rope sponges and lots of gray candelabra sponges. Just drift down over the fairly sheer slope and enjoy the fish life. Currents are normally mild, but can be strong at times.

The reef itself has a nice selection of hard corals. Deeper down you will find plate corals and areas of ship corals. Black coral also grows in the deeper reaches on the reef. As the dive ends, enjoy the coral near the drop-off, where sea fans can be spotted. The area closer to the land is sandy and may have a ray or two. The water on this reef is normally extremely clear, and you can see the boat clearly from 100ft.

This is a beautiful dive at reef top and over the sloping wall. The mooring here sits in 20ft of water. The inner flats are sandy and the outer flats to the drop-off have nice coral growth, including clusters of sea rods, sea fans and vase sponges.

Dolphins have been seen hunting for food in the sand in these shallows. From here to **Forest** dive site, this costal area is considered good snorkeling by the marine park.

Over the reef, the coral cover becomes competitive with star and finger corals and some plate corals. It is a very fishy reef with a hidden cleaning station among the rods and sea whips. Look for tiger grouper, trumpetfish, barred hamlets, rock beauties, blue tangs, honeycomb cowfish, lots of stoplight parrotfish and curious French angels.

Explore the soft corals and sea fans in the sandy upper reef while decompressing, and look for flamingo tongues on the bases of the sea plumes. The reef top also has a few very well formed candelabra tube sponges.

Creole wrasse are found on most Bonaire reefs

Sea Turtles

The people of Bonaire love sea turtles. They even have some that are tagged and have been given names, and the local newspaper prints updates on the tagged turtles' progress. Sea turtles, including their nests and eggs, are protected by both local and international law, as they face extinction worldwide. Nearly all Caribbean turtle populations are severely depleted.

Klein Bonaire's sandy beaches are nesting grounds to hawksbill and loggerhead turtles. Bonaire also has green sea and lunker leatherback turtles in its waters. Divers are asked to report sea turtle sightings and look for the turtles with tags on their front flippers. Report forms are available at local dive shops. As the beaches on Klein Bonaire are nesting areas, visitors are asked to avoid walking through the dunes or any area that is marked off, as this is where turtles make egg nests.

There is an organization called the Sea Turtle Club of Bonaire that can provide information. The phone number is ☎ 599-717-8399. The sighting network is very successful and visitors are encouraged to participate.

H   MONTE'S DIVI

Location: *Klein Bonaire*
Depth: *20-120ft (6-40m)*
Access: *Boat*
Range: *Novice*

Divi is the local name for a tree which sits on the shore of this site.

The reef top near the beach has large brain corals and numerous blue chromis that make the reef come alive with their electric blue colours. Divers can get right to the drop-off as the mooring is in 30ft of water and the slope drops off sharply. Look for various angelfish, multiple species of parrotfish, surgeons and even Nassau grouper. Lizardfish or sand divers like to rest on the plate corals found down about 50ft to 60ft along this reef.

Sponges here aren't particularly large, but there are plenty to see, including bright red rope sponges, tubes sponges and some orange elephant ears. This reef has some excellent growths of smooth flower coral. In the shallows you may see a lot of sea plumes with flamingo tongues on them. Also, look in the sand for live sand dollars.

I   ROCK PILE

Location: *Klein Bonaire*
Depth: *20-110ft (6-24m)*
Access: *Boat*
Range: *Novice*

This site is named after a rock pile on the beach. Below the sea, the reef is good for snorkelers and divers who enjoy lots of poking around in the shadows. The sand is almost as white as snow and the brain corals and sea plumes make this a

A hermit crab pokes from its shell

beautiful site to explore. The mooring is fairly shallow here and the corals below the boat can be appreciated by snorkelers or adventurous kayakers.

This reef is good for eels, both spotted and green. Sea turtles have also been observed and there is nice star and boulder coral.

The next few sites are getting into the normally calm and protected part of the island, and they are good for night dives. Look for big channel-clinging crabs in the reef. The light illuminates the bright red shells of these creatures as they venture out of their daytime hiding places, Octopuses scour the reefs as well. There

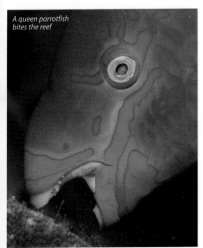
A queen parrotfish bites the reef

are some nice yellow line arrow crabs in the sponges. This is an interesting spot for night exploration where you don't have to go very deep and there is a good variety of marine life.

J JOANNE'S SUNCHI

Location: *Klein Bonaire*
Depth: *15-130ft (4.5-40m)*
Access: *Boat*
Range: *Novice*

The local joke is that all of the reefs with female names were past girlfriends of the charismatic Capt Don, and apparently Joanne was memorable for her *sunchi* (kiss). It's a pretty name, whatever the origin, and the reef below is nice as well.

The corals here are diverse. Head down the mooring in only 15ft of water and have a good look at the upper reef with various sponges, sea fans and sea plumes mixed in with small corals.

The drop-off has black durgons, chromis and wrasses swimming along the reef. The sandy channels heading down to the deep water break the reef up. The sponge life is also good here. Sea turtles are also seen along this stretch of reef.

K CAPT DON'S REEF

Location: *Klein Bonaire*
Depth: *15-130ft (4.5-40m)*
Access: *Boat*
Range: *Novice*

The top of the reef is shallow where the mooring is, but it's mostly sand. Sometimes this nice white sand is referred to as sugar sand. When the corals get thicker near the drop-off, they have some beautiful formations and interesting residents including French grunts, purple-tipped anemones with commensal shrimp and swaying sea fans. The sand is home to peacock flounder.

This reef has a series of points and ridges and some interesting sponge life. Many spots have beautiful settings of tube sponges along with the orange elephants ears. The elephant ear sponge is often highlighted by beautiful fairy basslets. Some of the hard corals, in the 60ft and below range, have been overgrown with some coralline algae. Wire corals, sea rods, sea plumes, rope, tube and vase sponges all populate the slopes.

The reef has a series of points and valleys; the points being good places to look for fish life, as the gentle currents roll over the reef. There are gray angels, bicolor damsels and marauding wrasses.

Tucked into a south bay, this is also an excellent night dive. Look for frogfish in the rope sponges.

A scarlet lady shrimp cleans a smooth trunkfish

L SOUTH BAY

Location: *Klein Bonaire*
Depth: *23-120ft (7-37m)*
Access: *Boat*
Range: *Novice*

This is a nice upper reef that is quite landscaped, leading some divers to describe it as an aquarium. The shallows are good enough for a long shallow dive, and also for snorkelers. At this site, you'll see lots of white sand, scattered corals and lots of small fish.

There is a chance to see bigger fish here including Nassau and tiger groupers over the drop-off. Horse-eye jacks, barred jacks and an occasional barracuda coast in.

Sponges and hard corals make up an interesting terrain down the slope. This can also be a pleasant night dive.

M HANDS OFF

Location: *Klein Bonaire*
Depth: *20-110ft (6-37m)*
Access: *Boat*
Range: *Novice*

The mooring here is in shallow water and divers tend to enjoy the dense coral growth that runs all across the reef flat and down the slope to about 120ft.

The sponge life is worth seeing as there are big, orange elephant ear sponges and nice tube and candelabra sponge formations. It is a good reef for macro-photographers and wide-angle as well.

Look for gray and French angels, groupers and wrasses. There are a lot of cleaning stations here, so look for fish lined up to get a cleaning. Since so

A tiger grouper at Forest

many things come out of the coral here at night, this is a good place to go after dark.

N   FOREST

Location: *Klein Bonaire*
Depth: *20-110ft (4.5-40m)*
Access: *Boat*
Range: *Novice*

This little rocky peninsula is considered to be one of the premier sites at Klein Bonaire. It is one of few sites close to a sheer drop-off in Bonaire and there is a forest of black coral trees that give it its name.

This is a popular dive, and dive boats jockey for position to get to the mooring first. Talk your guide into leaving early so you can be first to the mooring and be sure not to miss this site.

This site is a good place to look for sea turtles and is also famous for its elephant ear sponges. There's a small cave that may hold a grouper or two

along the steep reef. Lots of coral-cover make this a great place to poke into the recesses and look for cleaning stations. This site is also very fishy and schooling fish like grunts, chromis and even jacks come around all the time.

It is on the tip of the southwestern corner of Klein and wind can sometimes be a major factor here, making it hard to get to the mooring and stay on the mooring. But if conditions are right, this is one of the must-do dives for a Bonaire trip.

O   SOUTHWEST CORNER

Location: *Klein Bonaire*
Depth: *22-130ft (7-40m)*
Access: *Boat*
Range: *Novice*

This reef created a buzz in 2005 when a big loggerhead turtle was found swimming here and was tagged by conservation volunteers. Aside from being a good spot to see sea turtles, hawksbills being more common than loggerheads, this is a healthy reef flushed by currents that run around the point.

The mooring sits a bit away from the shore in 22ft of water. While not tabbed by the park as a snorkeling site, snorkelers do like the coral growth in close to shore. The reef has sea fans and also sea rods and large sea plumes. Schooling grunts and male and female stoplight parrotfish are seen here.

The slope isn't as extreme as **Forest,** but it still has lots of life and is very fishy. Divers have seen some immense green morays here. Watch the currents; they can get strong from **Forest** over to **Munk's Haven**.

P	MUNK'S HAVEN

Location: *Klein Bonaire*
Depth: *20-110ft (4.5-40m)*
Access: *Boat*
Range: *Novice*

Another good dive flushed by currents, black durgons and other mid-water fish, making for an interesting reef for fish lovers. The mooring is in 20ft of water and while the park does not recommend this site for snorkelers, many snorkelers and shallow divers love the reef top here. There are many soft corals up top and scattered coral heads.

Over the reef, the corals get bigger and the formations and competition for space makes for some nice coral heads with lots of spaces for barber pole shrimp and other cleaners. Look for tiger groupers and down deep for the large Nassau grouper that are sometimes seen here. This is another good site for turtles.

Divers must keep an eye on the current at times, and the directions of the guide. When they get strong, divers have been known to drift from here to

Forest, covering three dive sites at once as they whisk around the point. This is a rare occurrence, but you still need to be aware while you're diving.

Q	TWIXT

Location: *Klein Bonaire*
Depth: *30-130ft (9-40m)*
Access: *Boat*
Range: *Novice*

This site is currently closed to diving and snorkeling.

A Pederson cleaner shrimp awaits action

R SHARON'S SERENITY

Location: *Klein Bonaire*
Depth: *18-110ft (5-34m)*
Access: *Boat*
Range: *Novice*

Sharon's Serenity is close to **Southwest Corner** and has a similar dive profile. The mooring is in 18ft of water with some hard and soft corals in the shallows and then sloping down. Currents aren't too much of a worry, but they can pop up.

This coastal area was hit by storm waves from Hurricane Lenny in 1999, and this side of Klein suffered the most damage. At one time, Sharon's Serenity had plenty of elkhorn and staghorn corals in the shallows and a variety of soft corals, however these have somewhat thinned out now. If you had not been here before the hurricane, then you won't know the difference. New corals are starting to grow and the rubble possibly holds a greater variety of fish than before. Sometimes these ocean disturbances change the nature of the reef and that can be to the diver's benefit when new species move into new areas.

Brain corals, lobed star corals and other hard coral formations can be found along the drop-off and this is a favorite spot for small tropical and hawksbill turtles.

S VALLERIE'S HILL

Location: *Klein Bonaire*
Depth: *20-130ft (6-40m)*
Access: *Boat*
Range: *Novice*

This site is currently closed to diving and snorkeling.

Sea rods along the wall

Sponge life at Klein Bonaire is very healthy

| T | **MI DUSHI** |

Location: *Klein Bonaire*
Depth: *20-130ft (6-40m)*
Access: *Boat*
Range: *Novice*

This is a good place to look for rubble at the den of an octopus, and then see if the creature is around. Seahorses have also been found in the shallows on this reef. With the mooring in 20ft of water, this is a good dive for all diving levels. The shallows have hard corals including staghorns and some finger corals. The reef top has many juveniles in the shallows.

Over the reef, look for sponge-life such as orange-yellow branching vase sponges. There are also smaller purple tube sponges here with small gobies inside. Hard corals along the reef include great star coral, mountainous star coral and hill coral.

Some flower corals are also found at Mi Dushi. This is a good Valentine's Day dive, as *Mi Dushi* is Papiamento for 'my sweetheart.'

| U | **C H ANNEX / YELLOWMAN** |

Location: *Klein Bonaire*
Depth: *20-130ft (6-40m)*
Access: *Boat*
Range: *Novice*

This site is currently closed to diving and snorkeling.

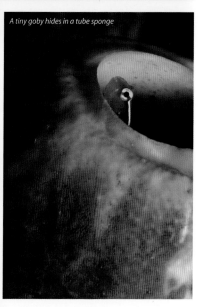
A tiny goby hides in a tube sponge

V CARL'S HILL

Location: *Klein Bonaire*
Depth: *20-130ft (6-40m)*
Access: *Boat*
Range: *Novice*

This site is named after Carl Roessler, an accomplished underwater photographer and the man who is given much credit for starting live-aboard diving and properly organized dive travel. He made many of the first visits to what are now diving's hot spots, and when he dived at this site a few decades ago, he was given a little bit of Bonaire.

There is a true vertical wall on this site that divers truly enjoy – adorned in hard and soft corals, tube sponges, tubastrea coral and lots of other colorful marine life. While cruising this wall, look up through the clear water through the corals and you can see the sky. The wall runs from about 25ft to 80ft and is worth a nice, slow swim to take in everything that lives here.

This wall is a great spot for any type of underwater photography. Look for blue parrotfish, cruising jacks, groupers and a barracuda or two. Seahorses have been reported in the shallow parts of the reefs.

W EBO'S SPECIAL

Location: *Klein Bonaire*
Depth: *17-120ft (5m-37m)*
Access: *Boat*
Range: *Novice*

Considered one of the best sites in this area, it is named after one of the local pioneers and ambassadors of the Bonaire diving scene, Ebo Domacasse.

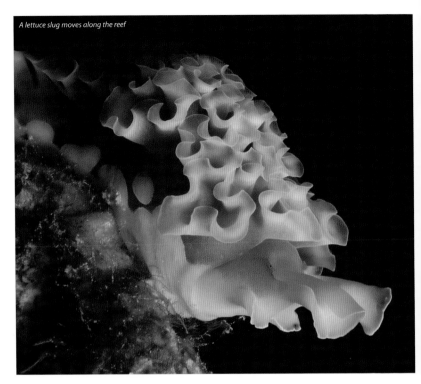
A lettuce slug moves along the reef

In fact, he is considered so special to Bonaire diving that he has not one, but two dive sites at Klein Bonaire bearing his name. **Ebo's Reef** and **Ebo's Special** pay homage to a guide known for his quiet and relaxed ways and an unselfish dedication to building the industry. He was awarded the reef names, according to Capt Don Stewart, 'as a sign of respect and love from other guides, as well as from his divers.' And the legacy continues, as one of Ebo's sons is currently a high-placed government official on Bonaire.

This reef has a collection of hard corals and something special in the form of a small cave that holds occasional groupers or nurse sharks, plus coneys and tiger groupers. There are some cleaning stations here in the 45ft to 65ft range active with chromis and queen parrotfish.

Both **Ebo's Special** and **Leonora's Reef** have shallow moorings and snorkelers like to explore the reef areas of both sites.

X	LEONORA'S REEF

Location: *Klein Bonaire*
Depth: *16-130ft (5-40m)*
Access: *Boat*
Range: *Novice*

If you want lettuce sea slugs, you've come to the right place. This is a wonderful site for macro and fish life with good coral cover and some huge coral heads. The large amount of lettuce slugs and the chance to see other nudibranchs may be due to the aftermath of

Hurricane Lenny, which stirred up the area and allowed some algae to grow on damaged corals. This is a real bonanza for macro buffs as the critters are plentiful.

There are also great opportunities to shoot some slender filefish that like to hide in the branches of the sea plumes and other soft corals. Bristleworms also like to crawl in the branches of these plumes.

The hard coral is in the 40ft to 60ft area and below. Look also for rope sponges, gobies crawling around tube sponges and squirrelfish hiding in the corals.

Y KNIFE

Location: *Klein Bonaire*
Depth: *20-100ft (6-30m)*
Access: *Boat*
Range: *Novice*

This site was closed for a long time and re-opened by the park in 2006. Currents are normally negligible to mild, and diving can be done from the buoy at 20ft down to 90ft to 100ft.

There is good coral cover on the reef at this site. Butterflyfish species such as the banded butterflyfish can be seen, and four-eye butterflyfish can also be found. Look out for rock beauties, gray angels and – if you're lucky – queen angelfish.

The upper reef area is good here with schools of grunts. The soft corals also provide cover for some juveniles like narrow trumpetfish that blend in good camouflage.

Keep an eye out for hermit crabs carting along a shell. If you wait long enough, the crab will tire of hiding from you and come out. The crabs are usually bright red and make very good photo subjects.

Z SAMPLER

Location: *Klein Bonaire*
Depth: *28-110ft (9-34m)*
Access: *Boat*
Range: *Novice*

Divers like this spot as it gives a sample of most everything one might find on Bonaire and Klein. This site is good for day and night diving and the deep mooring buoy gets the diver right over the reef and ready to see the marine life. Since it is near the daytripper sites, the fish here have been fed and they may follow you around. If you think a French angel likes your new dive gear, you're probably wrong – it wants a piece of bread.

At night, divers have reported sleeping sea turtles and a huge loggerhead was even seen here at one time. This site is good for lobsters and crabs at night as well, and frogfish are also found on the reef. Look in the bigger holes and deep water for large Nassau grouper.

This is one of those dives that every level of diver seems to enjoy and can be rewarding for macro photographers.

Flamingo tongue shell with mantle out

Marine Life

Pufferfish mate at the reef top

Boasting the largest fish population in the eastern Caribbean and an equally diverse invertebrate population, Bonaire is a superb place to get to know the ocean and its creatures. Most fish, crabs and other marine creatures have specific habitats. Finding out where a certain subject likes to live, when it feeds, when and where it mates and all of the other routines of life under the sea will enable the diver to locate the subject with greater ease. This enhances observation and also photography.

Colorful fish are perhaps the most sought after in the Bonaire waters. Beautiful angelfish, parrotfish, basslets and triggerfish all catch a diver or snorkeler's eye. But there are more mundane fish also worth watching for their unique coloration and ability to camouflage, like a seahorse or frogfish.

The invertebrate world around Bonaire can't be dismissed. The amazing sponge formations on virtually every dive site give the reef form and color. Bonaire's corals are healthy and very competitive, sometimes growing into or on top of one another. And the crustaceans like shrimp, crabs and lobsters all have unique homes and many have symbiotic relationships with other marine creatures.

Below is a small sampling of some of Bonaire's special undersea life.

HAZARDOUS MARINE LIFE

The diversity of marine life extends also to dangerous marine animals. Most of these are quite small and not ferocious, but highly venomous. There are cone shells, scorpionfish, stingrays, hydroids, fire corals, urchins and many other marine creatures that adversely affect a diver.

Divers should read or ask about which will be commonly seen and should know first aid procedures in the rare event a person is wounded by a marine animal. Be especially careful on night dives. Carrying proper antiseptic ointments greatly helps.

Sharks

Sharks are encountered on few dives in Bonaire. Attacks are rare and usually only occur in some misguided feeding attempt, or on fishermen illegally spearing fish. In the event a shark does become aggressive, it is sometimes wise to rise to a shallower depth to get out of its territory. If a shark comes too close, stop and face it while watching closely and quietly. Be prepared to push it away with a camera, knife, spear or tank. Treatment for bites is to stop any bleeding, reassure the patient and treat for shock and seek immediate medical treatment.

Bristle Worms

While they may seem soft and fluffy, they can deliver a painful sting. Each of the bristle worm's body segments has a pair of small parapodia, or paddle-shaped appendages. These have embedded tiny hairs or bristle-like pieces. They have well-developed sense organs with a kind of head with eyes, antennae and sensory palps. If stung, pick out the hairs using tweezers or duct tape and submerge the sting in very hot water for 30 to 60 minutes. If the victim has a history of venom allergies, seek immediate medical treatment.

Bristleworm with painful bristles

Fire Coral

It looks pretty with its caramel color, but touching fire coral is like putting your hand on a lit cigarette. It actually has tiny 'hairs' that burn like crazy and can swell up afterward. This mechanism is to defend against munching parrotfish, but divers sometimes get tagged as well. If stung by their powerful nematocysts, the skin will burn and itch. Rinse with seawater or water and apply vinegar or methylated alcohol on the sting. In a severe case anti-histamines can help but seek immediate medical treatment.

A diver observes a giant green moray eel

Jellyfish

The stings of a jelly are released by nematocysts contained in the trailing tentacles. The rule of thumb is the longer the tentacles, the more painful the sting. Keep an eye out for jellyfish in the Lac while snorkeling. On the outer reefs, man-o-war and sea wasps are found. Most stings can be treated with vinegar. Some people do react adversely to jellyfish stings, similar to those who are allergic to bee stings. Be prepared to administer CPR and seek medical aid.

Barracuda

Barracuda bites are also quite rare. The fish tend to be attracted to shiny objects and have been known to attack in murky water. Like sharks, this is normally a case of mistaken identity and invariably an accident.

On Bonaire's reefs, small schools and individual blackbar barracuda will frequently be encountered. There are also a lot of larger great barracuda. These fish should not be teased. Their bites can be damaging, so stop any bleeding, reassure the patient, treat for shock and seek immediate medical treatment.

Spotted Scorpionfish

These fish will be seen commonly in sandy and rubbly areas in Bonaire's waters and on night dives. They inject venom from spines on their back. The wound can be quite painful with a lot of swelling. To treat, wash the wound, immerse in water as hot as the victim can stand for 60 to 90 minutes and seek medical aid.

Sea Urchins

These spiny critters can be a real problem. The stings from the spines can range from irritating to highly intense. Spines can also break off inside the skin. Avoid contact with urchins, which means being vigilant in the areas they frequent, especially at night.

Treat by administering CPR until the pain subsides. Seek medical advice and use antibiotics where advised. In some cases spines may have to be surgically removed.

Diver and great barracuda

Coral Facts

A giant anemone sits atop a coral reef

1   Be aware that we use the word 'coral' for three things: the individual coral animal, called the polyp; the polyps and the skeleton they've secreted, also called a coral head; and the skeleton without its living polyps, also called coral rock. The first two of these are alive, the last is not alive, which leaves a great deal of room for confusion.

2   A coral polyp (the living coral animal) is only three to four cell layers thick.

3   To create a model of coral tissue against its own skeleton, take a wet tissue and drape it across a bare razor blade.

4   Every individual coral animal in a coral head is a clone of every other coral animal in that coral head.

5   A coral head is started by a single coral larva, which grows, and begins to secrete a calcium-based skeleton, and clones itself, and repeats the process. Slowly.

6   A hemispherical coral head 3in across is 200 to 300 years old.

7   The branching corals – elkhorn and staghorn – grow more quickly than the 'head' corals, such as brain coral and star coral. They thrive in shallower waters, though, so are more likely to be broken by wave action.

8   Look at a star coral head, or a starlet coral head: every single little mound or indentation – every single little circle in the whole coral head – is an individual coral animal.

9   Look at a brain coral head, or a sheet coral: the polyps aren't as easy to distinguish as they are in the star corals, but a careful look will reveal the mouths of the polyps, daytime or night-time.

10 The tissue of every coral polyp in a coral head is connected to all the polyps around it. The entire surface of a coral head is covered with living coral tissue.

By Dee Scarr

Travel Facts

Bonaire's motorcycle club members watch the sunset at White Slave on thier Sunday ride

GETTING THERE

Many international airlines service Bonaire on a daily basis. There is one-stop service (via San Juan, Montego Bay, Aruba, or Curaçao) from the United States and non-stop service from Europe (Amsterdam) as well as from Ecuador and Peru. The hot pink Flamingo Airport has a runway of more than 1.5 miles (2.9km) in length, long enough to accommodate 747 Jumbo Jets. The airport's designation is BON.

American Eagle has five nonstop flights from San Juan, Puerto Rico, to and from Bonaire each week connected via Boston, New York, Newark, Philadelphia, Baltimore, Chicago, Atlanta, Ft Lauderdale, Miami and Los Angeles. Divers have had problems with theft of expensive camera and dive equipment going through San Juan and complaints to the airport management don't seem to be heeded. Anything of value should be hand carried if going through San Juan until the blatant theft is addressed. Luggage sometimes gets delayed here as well.

Air Jamaica flies to Bonaire via Montego Bay on Saturdays.

One great new US option, which we took when researching this book, is the Continental Airlines weekly nonstop round trip flight between its Houston hub and Bonaire. Flight 1898 departs Houston on Friday at 11:30pm, arriving in Bonaire on Saturday at 6:15am. The return flight, 1899, departs Bonaire on Saturdays at 8am, arriving in Houston at 10:50am. Continental Airlines uses a Boeing 737 airplane with 124 (tightly packed) seats including 12 (more spacious) first class seats. The flight is a direct shot, avoiding the less dependable and theft-ridden stops. Continental Airlines is the world's sixth largest airline, so it connects in Houston to flights from all over the US and the world.

American Airlines flies direct, nonstop to Curaçao from Miami, and Delta flies there from Atlanta. Passengers then use either Dutch Antilles Express to connect to Bonaire. Flying time between Curaçao and Bonaire is approximately 15 to 30 minutes. Again, reports of delayed luggage come from this connection.

Another routing option is to fly on any of a number of major US and South American carriers to Aruba, and then take Dutch Antilles Express to Bonaire.

From Europe, KLM flies direct from Amsterdam to Bonaire up to twice daily. One flight continues on to Quito, Ecuador, and the other to Lima, Peru.

From South America, via Ecuador and Peru, the same KLM flights return to Bonaire with nonstop flights.

From Venezuela, nonstop charter flights from either Caracas or Valencia to Bonaire are available with PAS (Progressive Air Service). Additional service from Adventure Travel & Tours is available with nonstop flights between Caracas and Bonaire.

From Brazil, Varig and Avianca, fly from Sao Paulo and Rio de Janeiro to Aruba, which connect with Dutch Antilles Express.

From Colombia, Avianca has flights from Bogota to Aruba, which connect with Dutch Antilles Express.

If you are coming by sailboat, there is no anchoring allowed on the reef and moorings for visiting yachts are available on a first-come basis.

GETTING AROUND

An intricate network of good roads makes it easy to get around the island. Bonaire is not the most overbuilt island, which is part of its charm. The main roads are paved but don't always have centerlines. For the most part, Bonaire drivers are courteous and drive within the posted speed limits.

In some parts of the island, the road narrows to a single lane, like along the far southern beaches and also near some of the northern dive sites where the road runs along a cliff line. Here you must slow down and yield where appropriate. There are places to pull over. There are also some earthen roads.

The entire northern fifth of the island is national park and it is just about as natural as it can be. It is laced with one-way dirt roads that run along the shore lines and into the heart of the park. Although there are paving plans, a truck with high undercarriage clearance or 4WD vehicle is required here. You will not be allowed access with a conventional car.

Finally, many of the more central parts of the island, especially those east of Kralendijk and north of Rincon, are also unpaved. Rainy season is rarely wet enough to make roads impassable, but they can become muddy. The road near the mangrove at the Lac is one such road.

Bonaire has a good variety of rental options, including twin cab trucks from known names like Budget Rent-a-car, to small scooters, which can transport one person and snorkel gear. Many folks continue the Dutch tradition of bike riding as most of Bonaire is flat and easy to pedal around. If you're not used to the tropics, though, be sure to bring plenty of water.

Taxis are available but certainly not ubiquitous. Many hotels can arrange drop off in town and later pick-up for those wanting to remain unencumbered.

Some hotel packages even come with room, meals, diving and truck as part of the package. As shore diving is a lifestyle here, a good truck is a requisite for those who want pick their own favorite sites and not be part of the boat crowd.

Taxi drivers get a 10% tip as the norm. In dive shops and that sort of service, 10% is also the norm if your guides were attentive and helpful.

Catching some rays and wind at Lac Cai Channel

ENTRY REQUIREMENTS

Canadian and US citizens must have a valid passport and a return or ongoing ticket. A birth certificate with a picture ID is also acceptable for entry into Bonaire. Citizens of the Netherlands, Belgium, Luxembourg – along with any other countries with whom the Netherlands has reached an agreement on visa requirements – are allowed to stay up to 90 days (3 months) without having to apply for a visit extension.

Citizens of most countries in the world do not need a visa for their entry to Bonaire. Effective January 1, 2005, visitors from certain countries were required to have a visa for stays of up to three months (90 days) in the Netherlands Antilles. If you are not certain, call the Immigration Office of Bonaire (☎ +599-717-6880).

When you do come in you can bring articles for personal use. Visitors over 15-years-old are allowed 400 cigarettes, 50 cigars, 250g of tobacco, 2L of distilled beverages, 2L of wine.

The Netherlands Antilles has its own drug laws that are not the same as Holland's. Bonaire's drug laws are not at all lenient.

TIME

Bonaire is Atlantic Standard Time, which is the same as the US east coast during daylight-saving time (mid-spring to mid-fall).

Bonaire does not change time for daylight saving, as is the custom in the US and Europe. When it's noon in Bonaire it is 3pm (next day) in Sydney, Australia, 9pm in San Francisco, California, and 5am in London, England.

MONEY

The Netherlands Antilles guilder (NAFl) is the official currency. It is sometimes referred to as the floren. There are so many American tourists that the dollar is widely accepted. But expect your change normally to be in guilders. Oddly, the Euro has not become the major currency here, but can be exchanged at banks for local cash and dollars.

The guilder is fixed at the exchange rate of 1.77 to the dollar for cash and 1.78 for traveler's checks. Most stores and businesses exchange it at 1.75. You can spend dollars everywhere, but will likely receive your change in guilders. At the time of this book, the guilder is fixed on the dollar at a rate of FL$35 to USD$20 for retail transactions.

There are ATMs available all over the touristy part of Kralendijk and banking hours are 10am to 3pm, Monday through Friday. Traveler's checks are widely accepted. Be sure to have your passport or positive ID when changing traveler's checks at banks.

All of the major credits cards are widely accepted at hotels, restaurants, taverns and auto rental agencies.

TAX

Save some money, as when you are ready to leave there is a US$20 (35 guilders) departure tax at the Flamingo Airport for international departures and US$5.75 for flights to the other Antilles isles. But that's not all. There is a 5% tax on most goods and services (NAOB tax). Hotel room tax is US$5.50 to $6.50 per person per day. Car rental tax is US$3.50 per day. You'll see it on your bill or invoice.

ELECTRICITY

All electricity in Bonaire is 127 Volts AC at 50 Cycles (or Hertz/Hz). This doesn't really match either the power requirements of

Colorful home louvered window

The church at Rincon

Palms at a Bonaire condo complex

most European appliances (220V, 50Hz) or American appliances (110V, 60Hz).

A two-pronged wall socket similar to the US plug is used. Recent upgrades to the power grid make charging strobes, batteries and dive lights no problem. But it's not always clear what voltage the outlet is running at, so it's important to check this with your accommodation manager.

Many sockets do not have a third ground hole, so it is advisable to bring an adapter to make your cord plug two-pronged.

Many chargers, like the Ikelite super charger, come equipped to handle 100/240 volts and are fine. Most laptop computer power sources, like the Mac iBook, also have these. These are the handiest way to get your equipment charged up.

Most US appliances, like electric toothbrushes, will work but may just run a bit hotter. Some of the dive shops and resorts have stations for guest use for charging camera batteries and strobes. This may be a viable way to prevent problems with charging.

Most resorts are used to this problem and have transformers available for rent for your more sensitive items.

Transformers can also be bought in local stores such as Benzers, Inpo, and Playa Trading for $50 to $100.

Gadgets may be plugged into a 127V socket directly without a transformer, as long as you understand that some US voltage-specific devices may run warm, and may burn out if left plugged in for a long time. The best bet is to charge and then unplug. The author carried a power strip and if everything was charged, the strip was just unplugged.

Keep an eye on your room lights. If they start to go dim, unplug your stuff. Bonaire does occasionally have surges and brown-outs. If you plug anything electronically delicate into a wall outlet, it might not be a bad idea to have a small surge protector in between. You can bring these with you and they usually cost under $10. They are available at most consumer electronics stores, such as Radio Shack.

WEIGHTS & MEASURES

The system of metric weights and measures is used. Depths are registered in meters and weights in kilos. All sale and rental dive gear is oriented this way. See our quick conversion scale on the back inside cover.

TELECOMMUNICATIONS

Email outlets and Internet cafes are becoming more prevalent in Kralendijk Town. Many of the hotels have computers centers/business centers and a few even have wireless week-long packages. Email and Internet providers recently upgraded servers and service on Bonaire is now reasonably fast and reliable.

Some public places that offer you a web fix are BonaireAccess at the Harbourside Mall, Chat N Browse (a few blocks north of the mall) and Cyber City Webcafe (in City Café). Others are popping up.

The night scene in Kralendyk can be fun and lively

Captain Don's has a cyber café in the lobby as well and also wireless access for its guests with laptops.

If you are a subscriber to AT&T World-Net service, there is a Bonaire access number you can use. You pay the out-of-region access surcharge for the plan you are on.

TELEPHONE

Calls from Bonaire to the US are down-right expensive. While not a bargain, the Internet is certainly a much cheaper option. But if you do need to call to tell your jealous friends how good the diving is, a phone call from the hotel or resort directly is going to cost you between $3 and $4 per minute. Similarly, calls to various European countries are quite expensive too.

According to the folks at the tourism bureau there are four ways to get around this:
1 Go to the Telbo building in downtown Kralendijk, and call using phone booths (you pay at a nearby counter). This costs about half what the charge is at a resort.

2 Get a calling card from a long distance company which allows you to place credit card calls from Bonaire (check this with them first – it can be costly) Rates on calling card calls from Bonaire to other parts of the world vary depending on the card. If you plan on being on Bonaire for more than a few weeks and have your own number, you can use a callback service, such as that from TeleGroup.
3 Use an international calling public phone. There are 50 located around the island. Be forewarned these can also be very expensive.
4 Rent a local cell phone to use to make your overseas calls.

Telephone equipment on Bonaire is US standard, including the modular RJ-11 connectors. Telbo is accessible at ☎ 7000. Cellular phone service is offered by rentals from Cellular One as well as local service for your TDMA phone. It can be emailed (cs.cellularone@bonairelive.com) or via ☎ +599-717-8787. GSM is supported on Bonaire at European frequencies. Roaming with some carriers is possible as well.

If someone needs to get hold of you (or to make a direct hotel reservation) you can call Bonaire from the US or Canada by dialing 011-599-7XX-XXXX, where 011 is the international access code, 599 is the country code for the Netherlands Antilles, 7 is the city code for Bonaire, and XX-XXXX is the local Bonairean number you want to reach. If you were calling Bonaire from Europe or most of the rest of the world, you would dial 00-599-7XX-XXXX using 00 for the international access code. Recently Bonaire cellular numbers have been added and would be dialed as a normal Bonaire number.

Calling Bonaire from the US is about $1.50 per minute with no special rate plan. However, for a small monthly fee, most of the long distance carriers can set you up with an international calling plan that lets you call Bonaire for less than 45 cents a minute.

POSTAL

Local word is that the postal service is not overly reliable. Rely on FedEx or DHL if you are sending anything valuable or something requiring a timely delivery. For postcards, the local post office is probably fine and is located near the pier in downtown Kralendijk.

ACCOMMODATION

There are hotels for every budget and desire in Bonaire, but since most divers have equipment and expensive photographic gear, it is best to seek out the more upscale hotels to avoid any problems.

The most convenient dive hotels in Bonaire are right on the western shoreline. Many have 'dive and drive' packages that provide a certain amount of boat dives as well as vehicle for the popular beach diving. All have instruction and most have photo pros on the premises.

There are also many other options. Apartments, time-shares, villas, condos and even personal homes can be rented for those staying for a while or who want the comforts these provide.

Bonaire has a very active tourism association and is networked around the world. Places and packages can be perused on the Internet and reservations can be made online. Links can be found at www.infobonaire.com, which is the official site of the Tourism Corporation Bonaire.

There is a listing of diving centers at the back of this book. Many are affiliated with a hotel or have packages with hotels.

Lazing at the Plaza Hotel pool

DINING & FOOD

This is one of the few destinations in the world that gets a lot of tourists but doesn't have the fast food joints to match. There is a small KFC and a Subway, but that's about it.

There is no shortage of restaurants on this island and the food variety is also excellent, as is the quality of meals. There are Argentinean, Italian, Dutch, American, Bonairean, Mexican, Indonesian, seafood, vegetarian and international mix cuisines, just to name a few. They say there are over 70 cultures or cuisines represented on Bonaire. The majority of these eateries are found in Kralendijk or along the roads leading north and south to the various beach-front hotels.

A good number of the hotels also have their own bars and eateries and many are also varied in cuisine and quite good. Bonaire is arid and so most of the food is shipped in. This adds to the menu variety for a night out on the town.

For sure, one should sample local food. *Baka stoba,* a kind of beef stew, is delicious. It is also made with goat, chicken, fish and conch. The sign *Aki ta Bende Kuminda Krioyo* (local food sold here) is a good sign. The menu will have *sopi* (soups), *stoba* (stews) or food that is *hasa* (fried), and portions are generous and usually quite affordable. Some are pretty wild too. *Kabes ku higra* is goat brains and liver and *sanger* is fried blood.

Visitors may like *funchi* better. It is a starchy polenta mix that is quite tasty fried. Local food is served *pa bai kun'e* (to go) and to stay.

Tipping is much the same as in the States. Some restaurants add a 10 to 15% service charge automatically, so if in doubt, ask. The legal drinking age on Bonaire is 18 for both beer and other alcohol. The legal age for gambling in a casino is 21.

SHOPPING

The gift shops around Kralendijk and hotel dive shops have a colorful selection of goods ranging from the usual Caribbean fare of iguana T-shirts and wild do-rags to some very nice local art, mostly in the form of paintings. Landscapes, flamingoes, donkeys, tropical flora, seascapes, reefscapes…artists here tackle most every unique and colorful aspect of Bonaire. Some galleries and photo shops also offer a nice array of underwater photos and postcards.

There are some galleries as well. JanArT Gallery offers a weekly wine tasting every Friday where you can sip some fruit of the grape from 5pm to 7pm and meet some local characters, as well as see some of Janice Huckaby's Bonaire-inspired art. Galleries are small but interesting on Bonaire and most art pieces are originals, not prints or copies.

There are also some gold and silver stores that have nice pieces with an ocean and diving flair.

About once a week, a major cruise ship docks at Town Pier or the industrial wharf. Passengers disembark from 5pm to 7pm and the waterfront jumps with activity. Virtually all shops are open and the park across from Town Pier fill with vendors selling all kinds of artsy stuff. Beautiful photos, handmade bracelets and necklaces, drawings and paintings and lots of creative little knick-knacks can be found at these stands. It is worth heading into town after your morning dives to check out who has what for sale when the big ships come to town.

As for groceries, wine, liquor and snacks, there are some well-stocked supermarkets in town that sell fresh Dutch and American goods. They usually have a good selection of cheeses, sliced meats, fresh baked goods and other munchies that you can stash in the room for between-dive snacks and sundowners. Wines come from all over,

Fresh produce can be found at the waterfront market across from City Café

including South America, and are a good bargain. You can also buy Cuban cigars but Americans must enjoy them on-island as they are not importable into the USA.

Most stores are open Monday through Saturday from between 8 or 9am until noon, when they close for one to two hours, then remain open until 6pm. Hours vary widely and some stay open during lunch hour. The larger supermarkets are open from 7:30 or 8am until 7pm. These, too, may close during lunch. The place pretty much shuts down on Sunday but there may be some open for a few hours, like 11am to 2pm.

ACTIVITIES & ATTRACTIONS

There are plenty of things to do in Bonaire besides dive. In fact, tourism proponents are trying to promote Bonaire to not be thought of as 'just a dive destination' or a 'one-sport venue.' The consistent easterly winds have spawned some new sports here. Also, the natural beauty of the Lac Bay area, with its mangroves and dreamy shallow blue waters, is becoming popular. The Washington-Slagbaai National Park offers a lot to do in the form of hiking and biking. And, there are some pursuits that are gaining attention with the extreme adventure crowd.

Landsailing is fast and fun

Kitesurfing

This may be considered one of the more booming activities on Bonaire. The de facto hangout for kitesurfers is the sce-

---

Shell and Coral Products

The taking of shells and natural artifacts is strictly prohibited in Bonaire. Still, items using shells and marine creatures can be found. These are normally shipped in from places like Indonesia and The Philippines. These can often be seen in the form of products like bracelets and earrings. Divers are encouraged to discourage the creation of these products by not purchasing such items and telling storeowners that they disapprove of seeing these items on the shelves.

If you are offered a wildlife product or natural item for sale, ask questions about the product's origin. If the vendor seems poorly informed, think twice about your actions. Otherwise, your purchase could encourage continued illegal trade in wildlife, and be confiscated either before you leave Bonaire or on your return home.

When in doubt, don't buy and don't take. Leave it. Officials are quick to point out that anyone violating Bonaire's marine environment ordinance is subject to prosecution and heavy fines. The local motto: IF IN DOUBT – LEAVE IT OUT.

There is a real local grapevine that keeps an eye on environmental indiscretions and reports anything objectionable. Visitors are also encouraged to join this citizen watch. Report any infringements to the Marine Park office by telephoning ☎ 8444.

Passing a colorful store

nic **Margate Bay,** where the wind whips across the salt flats and fills the foils. This is a great place for learning the sport or practicing high jumps if you're good at it. The beach has a rustic old fisherman's hut and it is a good place to watch flamingoes commute as well. Some fishermen launch modest boats from the area too. Divers doing walk-ins at **Red Beryl** or **Margate Bay** should pop up a safety sausage here when coming back in from a dive to avoid being hit by a kiteboarder.

Windsurfing

In Bonaire, the wind is constant most of the year making the large and sandy shallows of the Lac area a favorite for all levels of windsurfer. Although one can traverse 8 sq km here, most of the action is at the southwest tip. Boards and sails can be rented from concessions.

Also, Jibe City, a bar with some nice food, may be the best hangout on Bonaire.

Land Sailing

Don't want to get wet? In Bonaire, no problem. Try land sailing. This is a unique sport just starting up in Bonaire. These wind-powered high-tech go-carts with windsurf sails rip around an oval or figure eight track that is located along the east coast on the way up to Rincon. Lessons and safety equipment are provided for this fast-paced sport, which is a good adrenalin rush. See www.landsailingbonaire.com.

Kayaking

The Lac Bay area is a wonderland of mangroves and odd sea creatures. Guided kayak tours are held here daily and people get to see endangered conch, sea turtles, small sponges and barnacles clinging to the mangrove roots, sea stars, bird life and lots of other things in this natural netherworld. A guide is recommended for this experience to ensure the fragile environment isn't accidentally damaged.

The sun setting over Klein Bonaire from Captain Don's Habitat

Kayaking can also be done at sea and people do kayak along the west coast and over to Klein Bonaire. You can snorkel from the kayak. This open ocean kayaking is best left to the experienced kayaker, but can be quite rewarding.

Sailing

Sailing is part of Bonaire's culture and past. Even the flag has a sailor's compass as part of its design. This is to show the navigation prowess of the early Bonairean seafarers. There is also a well-attended annual international sailing regatta every September. Many folks sail into Bonaire. It is a famous port for cruising sailors, and is known for its calm anchorage. But others prefer to be landlubbers and just go for a day sail or sunset cruise. This is certainly possible any day of the week on Bonaire and many cruises combine a morning of snorkeling and some fresh fruit or snacks. In the evenings a tropical rum or virgin punch can be part of a relaxing sail.

One unique ship is *Samur*, a vessel with a decided oriental flair supposedly built by a former CIA agent. The folks on *Samur* hoist the junk-style sails or let the guests give it a try. Full Thai dinners are catered on this ship.

Common but still endangered, the Prikichi is a small Caribbean parakeet

Another, the *Aquaspace*, was actually built as a research vessel for Jacques Cousteau. This futuristic trimaran, with below-deck reef viewing and day snorkeling venues, is a good way to see the reef. An evening wine and cheese cruise is also offered.

There are other more conventional sailing adventures and even a traditional Dutch ship. A fine way to spend a dry day waiting for that plane to come.

Cave Snorkeling

Bonaire has some inland caves that allow a look at some stunning stalactites and stalagmites. Snorkelers edge into the caves and find clear, cool water and underground wonderlands. Bats and blind shrimp reportedly live in these caves. Steps are being taken to limit entry to just a few caves so as not to disturb the bat population or the delicate balance in Bonaire's caves.

Lots to Do

Bonaire's menu of action and casual sports is rapidly expanding. Other activities available on Bonaire include biking and mountain biking, hiking, rappelling, 4x4 driving, fishing charters, historic tours, bird watching, parasailing, waterskiing, body boarding and many combinations of all of these activities.

WILDLIFE

Bonaire may appear to be arid but it has a nice selection of wild creatures, some amazing cactus forests, tropical flora and colorful birdlife. Although the island is small, so is the population and the wild creatures in the national park and the undeveloped parts of the island are worth seeking.

A good pair of binoculars and a telephoto camera lens will enhance the experience. The park and some bookstores and dive shops sell books about the ABC wildlife. And the park's rangers are very knowledgeable.

Flamingoes fly in from Venezuela at sunset

Washington Slaagbai National Park

The closure many years ago of two large ranches, locally called *kunukus*, helped form the Washington Slagbaai National Park in the north end of Bonaire. The park is huge, covering almost 25% of the island. It is mostly natural, with only spits of paving and no overnight stays allowed. The ranches were in the business of raising goats and aloe vera. As partially cultivated lands they quickly reverted to their natural state. You must have a 4WD or car with enough clearance to pass the roads. They will not let you in driving a passenger car. Unpaved dirt roads take you through miles of giant candle cactus, aloe vera, and divi trees. The park is open daily from 8am to 5pm, and no entry is allowed after 3pm.

Flamingoes

The flamingo theme is a big deal on Bonaire, starting with a pink airport that opens your eyes upon arrival. There are only four places in the world where flamingo colonies breed and Bonaire is one of them. There are two good places

A lizard eats a cactus fruit

Iguanas

You may see them in the top of candle cactus, you may see them trying to eat your lunch, or you may see them get onboard your boat. Locally called Bonairean squirrels, *yuanas* (Papiamento) or iguanas are a fact of life on the island. A full-grown male can reach over 7ft from head to tail, and they can move like the wind. Large older animals are a pale green to gray, while younger ones are a stunning lime green. They know how to choose food with the highest nutrition and eat only fruits and greens. Some people think male iguanas have a sexual magic as they have two penises. They are also a favorite ingredient in local soups and stews.

Wild Donkeys

Bonaire's donkeys are descendents of the past when salt and supplies were hauled between Rincon and the salt pans located in the south. Donkeys used to roam wild but have mostly been rounded up. They became frequent car accident victims and also were pretty much inbred. Now, just a few donkeys still roam wild.

to see Bonaire's flamingoes, although during the rainy season you can see them just about anywhere with a lot of standing water. One is at the Pekelmeer Sanctuary to the south. The other is at Lake Gotomeer, in Washington Slagbaai National Park in the north.

The best way to get a great photograph is to bring a telephoto lens of 300mm or more. On a good day, they will gather by the hundreds. The population of flamingoes island-wide ranges from 8000 to 15,000, depending on the season. The Flamingo Sanctuary is located within the salt pans on the southern end of Bonaire and it is strictly forbidden to enter there, but people often wait along the shoreline road to watch them come in or head off to Venezuela.

Only a few donkeys remain in the wild now on Bonaire

The majority of the donkeys can be found in the non-profit Donkey Sanctuary (☎ +(599-9) 560-7607) located just south of the airport. You can see donkeys here or spend a day on safari if you want to get out into their habitat. They still rescue wild donkeys and provide medical care, food, water and shelter for the nearly 300 donkeys on the preserve. They also offer education about and interaction with the donkeys for children of all ages. The donkeys are allowed to run free within the park but may be isolated if they require medical treatments. There is a small gift shop offering T-shirts, mugs and other stuff to support this ranch.

There is a foster-a-donkey program and fostering lasts for one year. Donations pay for food, medicine, worming every six weeks, and all other necessary care. US tax deductible donations can be made to the Donkey Sanctuary Bonaire.

Wild Goats

Goats are just about everywhere on Bonaire. They roam wild and are also-farm-raised. They are a favorite food of Bonaireans. Bonaire residents say that virtually every goat on Bonaire is actually owned by someone, even though you see them in the middle of nowhere. They have been hard on the plant life and wild goats are being rounded up through various efforts to give endemic plants a chance to rebound. Try one of the local dishes. They can be very tasty.

SAFETY

While the island is considered generally safe, reports of hotel and condo room break-ins (even at night when people are sleeping) and thefts are on the rise in Bonaire. Even hotels with posted guards and private grounds have had problems. Notices are normally posted

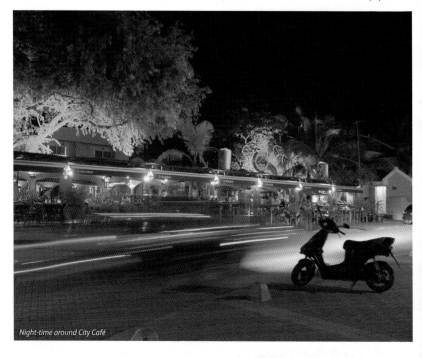

Night-time around City Café

A canal on the Plaza Hotel grounds

in the rooms and extra door locks and security pins are found at most hotels. But, sadly, some visitors do experience crime.

There is a reported cocaine problem locally that is said to be contributing to the rise in crime. There are far less reports of actual robbery or assault, but commonsense must be used in this regard as well. Try not to travel alone, and try not to stay out too late. Don't flash money around. Don't drink too much and become an obvious target. Use the same common sense and precautions you would in any unfamiliar place. It may seem like paradise, but that image can quickly fade if you let your guard down.

Shore diving is extremely popular here. A great number of divers rent pick-up trucks and just walk in at the many designated beach sites. The prevailing local advice is to bring nothing, absolutely nothing, of value along...just bring what you are going into the water with. Leave the vehicle open. Locking it will only invite the curiosity of thieves that would lead to broken windows. Some rental agencies insist on telling you to lock the vehicle, which goes against local advice. So get it clear with them in writing that if they insist you lock an empty truck, anything damaged or stolen (thieves sometimes open the

Snorkeling to see guests aboard Aquaspace

Colorful dive trucks sport marine themes on the island

hood and take a battery) as a result of criminals breaking into the vehicle is not your fault.

With only 13,000 people on the island, one would think the police would be more effective. This is affecting tourism to a certain extent so, hopefully, the crime issue will soon be addressed as earnestly as Bonaireans address reef protection.

RECOMMENDED BOOKS

Reef Fish Identification: Florida Caribbean Bahamas by Paul Humann and Ned DeLoach (New World Publications).

Reef Coral Identification & Reef Creature Identification by Paul Humann and Ned DeLoach (New World Publications).

Bonaire Shore Diving Made Easy Revised, A Practical Guide to the Shore Dives of Bonaire by Susan Porter (frequently updated, ask for the newest edition).

TOURIST OFFICES

Tourism Corporation Bonaire (☎ 599-717-8322; www.infobonaire.com; Kaya Grandi 2, Kralendijk, Bonaire, Netherlands Antilles)

Listings

BONAIRE DIVE OPERATORS

Selecting a Dive Operator

Question everything when looking for the dive operation with which you're going to spend your hard-earned holiday time and money. Get satisfactory answers about the operation you are planning to dive with, the type of equipment, type of boat and its maintenance, the divemasters, insurance coverage, cost of diving, knowledge of the travel agent you are booking with. Check the Internet as well. Send plenty of emails.

That said, it is comforting to know there are many reputable operators in Bonaire. But Bonaire's recent boom into tourism and the recent popularity of scuba diving means there are also a few shoestring operations where proper training and equipment maintenance is a secondary concern. For your own safety, peace of mind, value for the dollar and quality of holiday, it pays to be a wise consumer in Bonaire and anywhere else in the diving world.

Big Blue FreeDive Bonaire
☎ 9959
www.infobonaire.com/freedive/

Blue Divers
Kaya Norwega 1
☎ 6860
www.bluedivers.com

Black Durgon Scuba Center
Black Durgon Inn
PO Box 200
Email: Bonaire@blackdurgon.com
☎ 5736

Bonaire Dive & Adventure
PO Box 389
Kaya Gobernador N Debrot 77A
☎ 2229
www.bonairediveandadventure.com

Bruce Bowker's Carib Inn
PO Box 68
JA Abraham Blvd 46
☎ 8819
www.caribinn.com

Buddy Beach & Dive Resort
PO Box 231, Kaya Gobernador N Debrot
☎ 5080 (1-866-GO-BUDDY
US reservations office)
www.buddydive.com

Captain Don's Habitat
PO Box 88
☎ 8290 (1-800-327-6709 – US
reservations office)
www.habitatdiveresorts.com/bonaire

Caren Eckrich's Sea & Discover
Kaya Antonio Neuman # 11
☎ /Fax: 5322
www.seandiscover.com

Dee Scarr's Touch the Sea
Kaya Gobernador Debrot 133
☎ /Fax: 8529
www.touchthesea.com

Deep Blue View Divers
Address: Kaya Diamanta #50
☎ /Fax: 8073
www.deepblueview.com

Dive Inn Bonaire
Kaya C.E.B. Hellmund 27
☎ 8761
www.diveinnbonaire.com

Divi Dive Bonaire
Divi Flamingo Beach Resort & Casino
J.A. Abraham Blvd 40
☎ 8285 (1-800-367-3484
US reservations office)
www.diviflamingo.com

Great Adventures Bonaire
Harbour Village Beach Resort
Kaya Gobernador N. Debrot 71
☎ 7500 (305-567-9509
US reservations)
www.harbourvillage.com/html04/div-ing.html

Larry's Wild Side Diving
www.larryswildsidediving.com
☎ 5246

Ocean Adventures
Kaya Krisolito 10 (Santa Barbara)
☎ /Fax: 2278
www.oceanadventures.com

**Photo Tours Divers
(a division of Dive Friends)**
Kaya Playa Lechi #24
☎ /Fax: 2929
www.bonphototours.com
(www.dive-friends-bonaire.com)

Rec Tek Scuba
☎ 6537
www.rectekscuba.com

Renee Snorkel Trips
☎ 785-0771
www.reneesnorkeltrips.com

Scuba Vision
Kaya Grandi #6
☎ /Fax: 2844
www.scubavision.info

Toucan Diving
Plaza Resort Bonaire
JA Abraham Boulevard 80
☎ 2500 (☎ 1-800-766-6016
US reservations office)
www.toucandiving.com

Wannadive Bonaire
3 Locations: Eden Beach Resort:
Kaya Gob. N. Debrot z/n,
City Café: Kaya Grandi #7,
& the HUT: Kaya Dialma 11
☎ 8884, 3531, 8850
www.wannadive.com

**Yellow Submarine
(a division of Dive Friends Bonaire)**
Kaya Playa Lechi #24
☎ /Fax: 2929
www.yellowsubmarine.com
(www.dive-friends-bonaire.com)

Index

THIS IS NOT
THE END

www.lonelyplanet.com